DUTCH CINEMA

OTHER BOOKS BY PETER COWIE

Antonioni-Bergman-Resnais
The Cinema of Orson Welles
Eighty Years of Cinema
Fifty Major Film-Makers
Sweden 1 and 2
Finnish Cinema
Stars and Players
A Concise History of the Cinema (editor)
International Film Guide (editor)
World Filmography (editor)

DUTCH CINEMA

An Illustrated History
by PETER COWIE

London: The Tantivy Press
South Brunswick and New York: A.S. Barnes and Company
The Hague: Ministry of Culture, Recreation and Social Welfare

A. S. Barnes & Co. Inc.
Cranbury, New Jersey 08512

The Tantivy Press
Magdalen House
136-148 Tooley Street
London SE1 2TT, England

Library of Congress Catalogue Card Number: 79-63543

ISBN 0-498-02425-3

PRINTED IN THE UNITED STATES OF AMERICA

THINKING OF HOLLAND

Thinking of Holland,
I see broad rivers
languidly winding
through endless fen,
lines of incredibly
tenuous poplars
like giant plumes
on the polder's rim;
and sunk in tremendous,
open expanses,
the farmsteads scattered
across the plain,
coppices, hamlets,
squat towers and churches,
and elms composing
a proud domain.
Low leans the sky
and slowly the sun
in mists of mother-
of-pearl grows blurred,
and far and wide
the voice of the water,
of endless disaster
is feared and heard.

HENDRIK MARSMAN
(translated by James Brockway)

This book is dedicated to the
late S. I. van Nooten

CONTENTS

Note: the superior numbers in the text refer to books or articles cited in the Bibliography. Most other quotations are taken from interviews with directors or personalities, conducted by the author.

ACKNOWLEDGEMENTS

The author would like to acknowledge, above all, the aid, hospitality, and courtesy extended to him by the Film Department of the Ministry of Culture, Recreation and Social Welfare in The Hague (and especially G. J. van der Molen and Jan Kuper).

Many other individuals have given of their time and patience, knowledge and materials, recently and during the past decade. They include: Annette Apon, Nouchka van Brakel, Ronald Bijlsma, Ruud Bischoff, Hubert Bals, Jan Blokker, Charles Boost, Nico Crama, Adriaan Ditvoorst, Geoffrey Donaldson, Olaf Douwes Dekker, John Ferno, Louis A. van Gasteren, Bert Haanstra, Henk de Haan, Nikolai van der Heyde, Herman van der Horst, Rob Houwer, Hattum Hoving†, Jan Hulsker, Johan van der Keuken, Anton Koolhaas, J.N. Landre, Gé van Leeuwen, Charles Huguenot van der Linden, Rob du Mée, Piet Meerburg, René van Nie, S.I. van Nooten†, Pim de la Parra, Fons Rademakers, Piet Ruivenkamp, Jonne Severijn, George Sluizer, Jan de Vaal (and the staff of the Netherlands Film Museum), Paul Verhoeven, Wim Verstappen, Dick Vriesman, Jan Vrijman, Erik van Zuylen, Frans Zwartjes.

The 1,000th print of Bert Haanstra's award-winning documentary, GLASS

INTRODUCTION

As the plane glides in towards Schiphol Airport, the rectangular fields stretch like quiltwork beneath one. Columns of birch trees march away along the canals. Long greenhouses sparkle in the sun. Flatness is all.

Holland—or rather the Netherlands, as officialdom would have it—is so flat that the horizontal is the axiom in all its visual arts.

So flat that the serried ranks of the windmills could, once, relay news and messages as effectively as jungle drums.

So flat that the sudden, graph-like skyline of a town brings to the traveller an exquisite relief.

So flat that the true symbol of Holland is neither clog nor tulip—but the sturdy bicycle.

The landscapes of Jan van Goyen, Hobbema, Ruysdael and others give prominence to the Dutch sky; and the light of the Netherlands has inspired not only its painters but also its film-makers. Light that has a bloom and an eggshell-brightness. There are no rugged mountains, no rolling downs, to distract the realist's gaze. Perhaps this is why the Dutch have produced chiefly a documentary cinema. Life as it is, rather than life as it might be, remains their preoccupation. The exigencies of geography have animated the Dutch. Classics like Ivens's *New Earth* and Haanstra's *The Voice of the Water* are not mere descriptions of a struggle. They seek, and find, a compensating beauty in man's ceaseless combat with the sea.

Schiphol itself is below sea-level, reminding the visitor that he walks on reclaimed land. Bert Haanstra has built a studio facility in his own garden at Laren, not above but *below* ground level, in order to satisfy a municipal ruling that house extensions may not rise ugly from the soil. And to view the treasures of prewar Dutch film, one must plunge into the woods near the coast, at Overveen. There, beneath a bank of dunes, is set the vault, its nitrate cargo sustained by icy temperatures and careful custody by experts from the Netherlands Film Museum.

* * *

Dutch films have made their mark abroad because they are rarely parochial. They record the details of Dutch life and the pressures of existing in the most densely populated country in the world, but they do so with a wise and tolerant spirit that makes such observations fascinating to the outsider. Yachting is a sport particularly dear to the Dutch heart (even the word itself stems from the Dutch language), and yet Hattum Hoving's *Sailing* is a documentary that appeals to weekend sailors throughout the world. Such shorts depend on visual impetus; language is no hindrance to them. Dutch features, on the other hand, have long been handicapped by that linguistic barrier. The great figures in the literature of the Netherlands are virtually unknown beyond their borders: P.C. Hooft and Joost van den Vondel, those brilliant poets and playwrights of the Seventeenth century, or Multatuli, whose *Max Havelaar* has emerged as a remarkable film, or more recent writers like Simon Vestdijk and Henrik Marsman. The two literary giants that *are* celebrated—Thomas à Kempis and Erasmus—both wrote in Latin, not Dutch. As Kees Fens has commented, "Each Dutch prose writer has to start anew, since there is no established pattern for him to take as a starting point."[1]

Dutch cinema is also hampered by its lack of a dramatic tradition. Calvinism set its face against the establishment of a national appreciation of theatre; the Dutch still prefer to watch life than to forge its elements into drama. There are rewards, of course. It is hard for the Dutch to make a coarse-cut film. Their natural instinct is to formalise. Like good short stories, their documentaries have a beginning, a middle, and an end. They pivot jewel-like, gift-wrapped, on a point of universal truth; and are content with that.

There is a long tradition of patronage in the Netherlands, from which the Seventeenth-century painters and poets took profit. What one may legitimately look for and find wanting in Dutch cinema is the artist of Rembrandt's calibre who dares to depict his countrymen as they really are—and to be deprived of his subsidy for such pains. But in practice, the Dutch feature film has been in development for less than twenty years, and it may be that some Buñuel, Dreyer, Ray, or Bergman will arise at once to challenge and to praise his native land.

The Production Fund, financed by the Ministry of Cultural Affairs, Recreation and Social Welfare, has been more successful than such lopsided counterparts as the NFFC in England. The Fund also receives an annual grant from the Nederlandse Bioscoopbond, and in the two years 1976 and 1977, a total of 7.8 million Dutch florins was given in assistance to Dutch features. The Fund was established as long ago as 1956, antedating, for example, the Swedish or Danish Film Institutes' production schemes, but it really only began to take effect on the national scene in the later Sixties. All subsidies from the Fund are in the form of loans, amounting to between 30 and 60 percent of the total budget required to produce the film. The main condition of help from the Fund is that the producer in question should have arranged for the guaranteed distribution of his film once it is completed. The producer must then find the balance of the budget himself (with the aid, almost invariably, of the eventual distributor). The income from box-office receipts goes to the producer until such time as he has recovered his entire investment. The remaining revenue is divided between the Fund and the producer in proportion to the share each has made to the budget. Once the Fund has received up to 120 percent of its original loan, all remaining income accrues to the producer. The great advantage of the Fund is that it never forecloses on the unfortunate producer whose film may have proved a commercial disaster, whereas the friendly neighbourhood bank would pursue him with ruthless vigour.

Certainly it must be vouchsafed that the system of film subsidies in the Netherlands in no way impedes the growth of an artist; it is among the finest and most sophisticated systems in Europe, and without sponsorship the Dutch documentary as one knows it, and most of the new Dutch features, would be stillborn. The result for Holland has been a stream of international prizes during the past thirty years, from Herman van der Horst's award for *The Rape of a Land* at Locarno in 1947, to Nouchka van Brakel's success at the Cairo Film Festival of 1977 with *The Début*. Some shorts, like Haanstra's *Glass,* have circulated the world in thousands of prints; others, like Frans Zwartjes's experiments with light and sound, are coveted by festivals and film museums abroad but remain unseen beyond their doors.

* * *

This little book does not pretend to tell the entire history of Dutch film. Although I have been going to Holland annually for fifteen years, and have seen literally hundreds of Dutch films, my outsider's view must of necessity be no more than a survey of vital trends and achievements. My stress is laid on the postwar period, primarily because my readers will be more familiar with recent films, will have access to them, and will glean from them a more vivid impression of Dutch life and culture today than they would from the excavated reels of the Twenties and Thirties. By implication, my book believes in an expanding future for Dutch cinema. Most of the artists discussed are still young and active in the medium; some have still not reached their peak. There is no reason why the Dutch should not yield in the years ahead a cinema as bright and intelligent as the Australian or the Swiss.

Mannus Franken shooting the documentary MIAS-ARCHIPEL, in Indonesia in 1937

1. THE PIONEERS

As far back as the Seventeenth century, the Netherlands were involved in the development of cinematography. Cornelis Drebbel (1572-1633) experimented with a form of magic lantern, and Christiaen Huygens and Petrus van Musschenbroek also played their part.[2] Two hundred years later, Dutch cinema left the starting gate at much the same time as other Western countries, and in 1899 a costume reconstruction of William III's visit to the Vondelpark in Amsterdam (now, incidentally, the site of the Netherlands Film Museum) was filmed by the Nöggerath family. Anton Nöggerath Senior, who had owned a coffee shop in the Warmoesstraat in 1890, and who was already in show-business when the new phenomenon of cinematography arrived, soon made contact with Charles Urban and his Warwick Trading Company in England, and became agent in Holland for "The American Bioscope." A Dutch subsidiary of the American Biograph and Mutoscope Company, known as the "Nederlandsche Biograaf-en-Mutoscope Mij.," was also launched.

By 1901 or 1902, the brothers Albert and Willy Mullens, better known as travelling exhibitors, were producing short documentaries of local interest, and for the next twenty years the Hague and Hollandia studios churned out dozens of documentaries, newsreels, and melodramas. F.A.N. Film (Franz Anton Nöggerath Junior) made quite a number of fiction films between 1911 and 1913; Johan Gildemeijer's Rembrandt-Film produced one or two films a year from 1915 to 1918, all of them financially successful; and Theo Frenkel Senior's Amsterdam-Film was active from 1916 to 1921, with one or two releases a year.

This indigenous flowering was arrested on the outbreak of the Great War, for Dutch films could no longer be exported. The quality declined, in spite of co-productions with neighbouring England. By the late Twenties, and the advent of the talkies, the Dutch film was in a parlous state, and sound isolated the fledgling industry behind a linguistic barrier that for decades proved almost insuperable. On the exhibition side, however, great advances had been achieved, notably by A. Tuschinski, whose ornate cinema in the heart of Amsterdam was opened in 1921 and is still prestigious today.

During the Thirties, the common European demand for light entertainment in the face of economic crisis gave a brief impetus to Dutch cinema. Well-known directors were lured to Holland to work in the home language: Max Ophüls, for instance, Ludwig Berger, Douglas Sirk, and Henry Koster. The Cinetone Studios in Amsterdam, and Filmstad in The Hague, were built during this period. Arthouses like the Uitkijk in Amsterdam were flourishing. Rudy Meyer began to function as the best producer the country has ever had. There was even a film by Mannus Franken made in Indonesia, one of Holland's most important colonies, entitled *Tanah Sabrang* (1938), with a soundtrack in Malay, following in the wake of Franken's lyrical tribute to the region, *Pareh, Song of the Rice (Pareh, het lied van de rijst, 1936)*, a kind of Dutch *Song of Ceylon*.

As early as 1918, Dutch film importers and exhibitors united under the banner of the Nederlandse Bioscoopbond, which remains today a vital and influential organisation. Yet in spite of this activity, no tradition of Dutch-speaking cinema evolved. As Anton Koolhaas, a former director of the Netherlands Film Academy, put it, "The comparison is often made with Sweden. But apart from the earliest days, the Swedes were cut off from the flow of American and other foreign films. They could—and had to—make their own pictures in their own image." Others might argue that in other countries film was more securely entrenched in companies which controlled production, distribution, and exhibition (not so in Holland).

*   *   *

Nevertheless, in those distant days at the start of the century, the future looked bright for Dutch cinema. *The Adventures of a French Gentleman without His Trousers (Mesaventure van een Fransch heertje zonder pantalon op het strand te Zandvoort)*, made on a Saturday afternoon in July 1905, by Willy Mullens, with his brother Albert as cameraman, was long regarded as the "first" Dutch fiction film, but in recent years the research of Geoffrey Donaldson has proved that there were at least half-a-dozen shorts of this type made prior to *The French Gentleman*.[3] This brief comedy is still in excellent condition. The construction is tight and well-conceived, and the locations, on the beach and in the streets of Zandvoort near Haarlem, are brightly deployed. A staid French gentleman is dozing in his basket chair while the tide rises and gradually enwraps him. He has to tear off his trousers in order to stagger ashore, and is promptly pursued by a crowd of outraged spectators and police. The close-ups of the extras and bystanders are witty, and intelligently inserted by Mullens into the narrative, while the panning shots are sophisticated for this period. It is regrettable that the Mullens brothers, the first real showmen in the Netherlands, turned afterwards to documentaries and worked chiefly in the Dutch East Indies. There is a *brio* and an effortless visual flair in this early movie that eluded Dutch film-makers in later decades.

The great era of the Hollandia studios in Haarlem extended from 1912 to 1923 (almost exactly parallel in time to the flowering of the Swedish silent film), and *Two Girls from Zeeland* (*Twee Zeeuwsche meisjes in Zandvoort*, circa 1914) featured the celebrated Dutch actress Annie Bos, whom Donaldson regards as the only authentic film star Holland has ever had. The miraculous light that is at the heart of great Dutch paintings is immediately apparent here, as the girl-friends chat gaily with a dapper individual on board a tram; the sunshine floods in through the windows, bathing the composition with a realism similar to the unaffected location work in Verstappen's *Joszef Katús,* made half a century later (see Chapter Seven). The girls proceed to the seaside and paddle precariously. Their beaux overturn their basket chairs but, undeterred, the girls gird up their voluminous bloomers and wade into the surf. When they dance and frolic in front of the other holidaymakers, the local police intervene and chase them off the sands. Propriety wins the day again.

The Hollandia pictures were widely released, and their fame extended as far as South America. A feature entitled *Found Again* (*Weergevonden,* 1914) proves that the Haarlem team could tell a complex story too. Directed by Louis H. Chrispijn Sr. (one of the directors of *Two Girls from Zeeland*) and Edmond Edren, this is probably the only Dutch feature film to deal with the Jewish problems in Holland. Chrispijn himself plays the blind Jew who is driven out of his house with his younger daughter, and grows more and more impoverished. They load their pitiful chattels on a cart, push it through the streets of Amsterdam, and move finally into a rented basement room. But the film is enlivened by some neatly-timed comic sequences (such as the old man's tumbling into a canal after his dog has run off—with the result that everyone in cast and crew had to be revived with hot chocolate at the producer's house afterwards!), and the drama ends happily when the two daughters, long parted, meet again by chance as the husband of one of them, a doctor, comes to treat the other in the dingy basement.

Maurits H. Binger was the enlightened and enthusiastic producer at the Hollandia studios. By profession he was a book printer, but films obsessed him, and he devoted all his spare time to the development of his "Filmfabriek." There were numerous co-productions during this period, and *As God Made Her* (*Zooals ik ben,* 1920), based on a drama by Helen Protheroe Lewis, was typical of them, although the most famous at the time was *The Black Tulip,* co-directed by the American Frankland A. Richardson, and Maurits Binger. *As God Made Her* was directed jointly by Binger and the Englishman, B.E. Doxat-Pratt, under the banner of "Anglo-Hollandia Films, Haarlem," but most of the leading roles were played by English actors and actresses, with Dutch performers in the minor parts. The story is somewhat banal: a maid comes into a legacy and indulges in a spending spree to improve her social status. Through the good offices of Lady Muriel, "one of the best-known figures in the English aristocracy," played by Lola Cornero, she engineers an impressive marriage. But when her husband discovers her true identity and simple background, the maid leaves him so that he may make a fresh start, unsullied by this contact with the working class. She is pregnant, however, and bears a son; this reunites the couple, and after a space of three years husband and wife are seen happily together again.

As God Made Her is much more orthodox in style and tone than the films made by the Dutch in Haarlem. There is a wooden quality to the interiors, and the only interesting moments are afforded by the sunlit locations and a split-screen effect as the maid's husband remembers her seated on his knee. Less than three years later, Maurits Binger died, and the Hollandia Studios were closed.*

Into this vacuum of the late Twenties came the young Joris Ivens and Mannus Franken (see Chapter Three). Ivens is a little unfair when he writes in his autobiography that "the Dutch film industry up to this time had produced little more than a branch office of the international newsreel companies and some laughable screen repro- ductions of popular stage dramas, which we called 'movie dragons.' "[4] He thus ignores the accomplishments of the Hollandia studios, probably because he was depressed by the lack of good films during the Twenties. There were others apart from Ivens, too. J.C. Moll, for instance, a scientist who experimented with film in a tiny studio in Haarlem, produced *Crystals* (*Kristallen*, 1930), a micro-film that shows salt crystals expanding and changing shape in water, welling over the black background like preternatural plants or organisms. Only a fragment remains in the vaults of the Netherlands Film Museum. Otto van Neyenhoff emerged as a talent around this time, also, and his work was screened by the Filmliga. *The Sea* (*Zee*) is silent and comprises shots of the waves and the seashore, dunes swept by languorous winds, and immense skies rich in clouds. It is no more than a film essay, pursuing the same line of investigation into montage as Ivens's *The Bridge* (see Chapter Three), but it has a visual appeal that lingers long after its few minutes have elapsed.

The visit of Eisenstein to the Netherlands in 1930 was recorded by

---

*"The death of Maurits H. Binger and the closing of the Hollandia Filmfabriek did not immediately result in a stop in the production of Dutch films. In 1924 a new company, the Dutch Film Co., started working in the old Hollandia studio in Haarlem and made films until 1926, some directed by Theo Frenkel Senior, some directed by Alex Benno. Benno's own company, Actueel-Film, made folksy comedies from 1921 up to 1927. Another company, led by the actress Adriënne Solser, also made a film a year from 1926 to 1928 (which really did give the Dutch fiction film a bad name ... particularly at a time when the Filmliga movement was starting up)"—(*Geoffrey N. Donaldson, in a letter to the author*).

Hispano Film in The Hague, in the form of a newsreel shot and edited as the Master himself might have done, with close-ups of inanimate objects and a tongue-in-cheek wit as the camera follows Eisenstein on a trip round the most hackneyed tourist spots in Holland.

2. FROM THE THIRTIES, THROUGH THE WAR

One or two names apart from Ivens's are conspicuous in the Thirties. Jan Hin, for example, whose company produced several films with a Catholic theme, directed *Turn of the Tide* (*Kentering*, 1932), which traced the birth of the Catholic Workers' Movement. Starting in 1890, *Turn of the Tide* includes an excellent montage of factory routine. Even though the film is silent, one can *hear* the unremitting beat of the sledgehammers and the rasp of the hacksaw. The picture of poverty and malnutrition among the proletariat is moving, but Hin's intentions were finer than his cinematic gifts, and *Turn of the Tide* looks portentous and didactic today.

Mannus Franken was the central—if also the most modest— personality in the Dutch cinema of the Twenties and Thirties. He was the writer on whom the early films of Ivens really depended. He adapted Jef Last's short story, *Breakers,* into a screenplay; his was the inspiration behind *Rain* (as Charles Boost has written, the film is "loaded with melancholy and impregnated with a *tristesse* which must certainly be attributed entirely to Franken"[8]); and it was Franken whose passion for the French *avant-garde* brought a touch of sophistication to Ivens's style.

Franken was a humanist who felt that a documentary was incomplete without a human presence. While Ivens was fascinated by the abstract patterns and rhythms that could be achieved by the camera and in the cutting-room, Franken sought the poetic element in a blend of nature and human beings (e.g. his *Jardin de Luxembourg,* 1929). He was one of the founders of the first art house in Holland, the "Uitkijk" in Amsterdam, as well as the institutor of the Central League Films Bureau (Centraal Bureau van Ligafilms), a pioneering effort to preserve films properly. During the late Thirties, while in the Dutch East Indies shooting commissioned documentaries, Franken

Above: Gerard Rutten (beside camera) and the set of DEAD WATER

Above: still from DEAD WATER

Above: On location for YOUNG HEARTS

Above: tragedy strikes in YOUNG HEARTS

had an opportunity to make a feature almost entirely off his own bat. *The Land Across the Sea* (*Tanah Sabrang,* 1938) dealt with the emigration of the Javanese to the Outer Territories, and was enormously influential in Indonesia, from both a social and a film-making angle.

Gerard Rutten directed *Dead Water* (*Dood water,* 1934) from a screenplay by Simon Koster, and this altogether immaculately crafted film was clearly influenced by the Soviet style of the Twenties. The cinematography, which won a prize at Venice for Aandor von Barsy, is worthy of Tisse at his best, and the music was conducted by the great Willem Mengelberg. The theme of the picture is the closure of the Zuiderzee; a triumph of labour and ingenuity but a disaster for those dependent on salt-water fishing for their income. The hero is shunned by the villagers because he abandons the fishing community in order to work on the dike. In the taverns, disgruntled men gather to discuss the change that has overwhelmed their daily routine; they set out to dig and plough the land as an alternative source of livelihood. Rutten focuses on the faces in the lamplight, each set of features a marvel of character and rugged resolution. Out of doors, the images are impressionistic, luminous in their beauty. It is hard to believe, when one sees a film so mature and assured as this, that the Dutch cinema never leapt ahead before the war.

Another major achievement of the decade was the charming *Young Hearts* (*Jonge harten,* 1936), directed by Charles Huguenot van der Linden with the assistance of H.M. Josephson. There was no subsidy system in operation during the Thirties, and van der Linden devoted a legacy from his mother to the budget of the film, which was made chiefly on location. *Young Hearts* is ingenuous, almost naïve in its belief in human goodness, but it more than compensates for that with a jaunty pace, a lightness of tone, and a technical finesse rare in Dutch cinema at the time. A lonely woman, whose husband is forever away prospecting for oil, leaves her family and travels with her baby boy to the summer resort island of Texel. She is soon caught up in the frivolous antics of a student camp; an escapist romance beckons. The students are footloose and happy. One is a fanatical draughtsman; another plays the panpipes continually. Van der Linden draws the gossamer strands of this story together with consummate skill, as detectives arrive on Texel in search of the missing girl, and she is trapped by the deceptive flood tide. The holiday ends in tragedy, and there is the flavour of early Bergman (*Summer Interlude* or *To Joy*) in this loss of innocence, and in the sense of sun, sea, and wind playing their role in the drama.

In the same year, Max de Haas made *The Ballad of the Top Hat* (*De ballade van den hoogen hoed*), a lissome tale built on the notion of a top hat passing from owner to owner until it returns to the canal in which it began its journey, sailing along with stately *mien*. It is an idea frequently used by film-makers (one thinks, for example, of *Madame*

Two shots from THE BALLAD OF THE TOP HAT

de . . . , Lotna, and *The Yellow Rolls-Royce*), and de Haas brings such witty observation to bear on his locations and characters that one surrenders totally to the conceit. The hat is used at a wedding, and at a funeral. Atop a diplomat, it witnesses the destiny of great nations being decided at a mighty conference. It adorns a coachman and accommodates a workman's sandwiches. A black jazz trumpeter acquires it, but soon the hat is in the streets once more, kicked around like a football by some urchins until it sails with ineffable grace into the waters of the canal. There is nothing winsome or effusive about this little exercise in style. De Haas was always a believer in the *avant-garde,* and already in 1932 he had made an impact with *Torchlight Procession (Fakkelgang),* about teetotalism. He has been called the first neo-realist, and his appreciation of the Amsterdam streets and waterways is remarkably convincing, even today. His career, like that of so many artists, was cruelly cut in half by the Second World War. He was assigned to the Dutch East Indies, where he shot propaganda films about the threat from the Nazis and Japanese, and he spent three years in a Japanese internment camp. In 1947 he once again returned to the Dutch studios, and directed *LO-LKP,* a feature that enabled him to make full use of his flair for realism. Many of the actors in this story of the Dutch Resistance were re-living their own experiences. "LO-LKP" stood for the alliance between the organisation that helped Dutch people reluctant to go to Germany (and 400,000, apart from Jews, were ordered to travel there to work), and the actual Resistance squads. Some of the performances are clumsy, and there is perhaps too much emphasis on minor details. But certain scenes endure: the burial of a British pilot to the accompaniment of "God Save the King" on a rickety phonograph at the graveside; and the final execution, with bare young trees waving, flinching, as each salvo of shots rings out.

Max de Haas never relinquished the hope of finding new means of

Above: still from LO-LKP, directed by Max de Haas

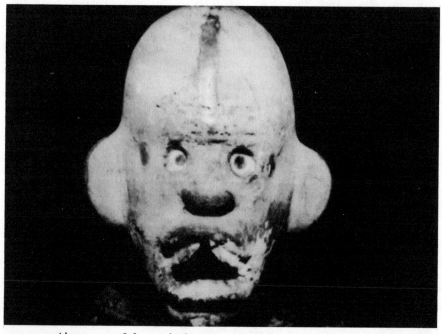

Above: one of the masks from Max de Haas's MASKERAGE

expression in film. Even *Maskerage,* a straightforward documentary about the Museum of Ethnology in Leiden, becomes a baleful journey into the world of tribal masks and statues, to the accompaniment of ferocious *musique concrète.* De Haas called on the same composer, Pierre Schaeffer, in collaboration with the young Michel Legrand, for *Days of My Years* (*Dagen mijner jaren,* 1960), which without dialogue offers a meditation on the act of human ageing and places its finger on the mysterious evolutionary process by which generation passes to generation.

* * *

Two of the most renowned "guest artists" in the prewar Dutch cinema were Max Ophüls and Ludwig Berger. Cinetone Studios financed *A Comedy About Money* (*Komedie om geld,* 1936), with a predominantly Dutch crew and cast apart from the great cameraman Eugen Schüfftan. Brand, the downtrodden hero of the film, works as a courier for a banking concern in Amsterdam, but is dogged by a dubious brother-in-law, who is constantly touching him for loans. Brand loses a vast sum of money belonging to the bank, and is promptly sacked. Creditors pursue him, his telephone is cut off, and he turns to drink and tries to commit suicide. Suddenly, salvation appears in the form of a remarkable offer: Brand is to be given the chairmanship of a new finance company, and overnight he is transformed into the mighty boss before whom all creatures bow and scrape. Of course, there is a catch in this newly-acquired serendipity, and Brand suffers another lapse from grace before he is finally accorded his freedom. Ophüls treats the story like an anecdote in a cabaret, and at start and finish, and occasionally during the narrative, a circus emcee comments sardonically on the action. It is a device that Ophüls was to use again in *Lola Montès,* that Bob Fosse relied upon in *Cabaret,* and that originated probably in Pabst's *Die Dreigroschenoper.* The professional verve and sleight-of-hand of Ophüls's Dutch film makes one wonder why it has been ignored for so long. The cutting is tart, too: as a big ball strikes the camera in a street, Ophüls cuts to Brand's daughter waking up, wondering what such a bang could mean, and then discovering that it is her father, returning home drunk. The film gives ample evidence of Ophüls's technical agility, including two successive 360° dolly shots around Brand as he launches a tirade against his brother-in-law (now employed as a doorman in the finance company). Ophüls satirises the romantic fashions of the period in *Komedie om geld,* and his screenplay contains one prescient, jet-black joke as Brand, the Jew, recalling his suicide attempt, says, "My memories of gas are not so good!"

Berger lacked the slyness and wit of Max Ophüls, but his 1937 version of *Pygmalion* was highly regarded at the time of its appearance, and *Somewhere in Holland* (*Ergens in Nederland,* 1940) was a kind

Germanic lighting in Max Ophüls's KOMEDIE OM GELD

of Dutch *In Which We Serve,* inspirational at the time and somewhat embarrassing to behold today. The mobilisation of 1939 caused an upheaval in the life of millions of people. Berger concentrates on one particular group, a lawyer and his attractive wife, and an actor who steps into the emotional breach while his friend is away minesweeping. The film is fast-moving, and the exteriors are finely used. But the image of life aboard ship in wartime is aseptic and outmoded, and belongs more to 1914-1918 than to the Second World War. Jan de Hartog still looks impressive, however, as the dashing young lawyer who becomes, *inter alia,* the bravest defuser of mines in the entire Dutch navy.

Only a few months after the opening of this film, the Nazis took over the Cinetone Studios under the banner of UFA, and it was not until 1948 that the Nederlandse Bioscoopbond could raise sufficient capital to re-open Cinetone. How ironic to note that in the ensuing Fifties it was more often than not German directors, such as Wolfgang Staudte and Georg Jacobi, who shot their films in this facility.

There were other sporadic attempts to take reality to a dramatic level, but most of them are best forgotten. *Six Years (Zes jaren,* 1946), made by H.M. Josephson with Charles Huguenot van der Linden, is an honourable endeavour, a tribute to the young men and women who had participated in the Dutch Resistance during the war. In the form of a lengthy flashback, it shows the impact of the Nazi invasion on the student generation in Leiden. The "Arbeitseinsatz" was a terrifying dilemma for the Dutch; while Germans were sent to the crumbling Eastern front, Dutchmen were drafted to work in German armaments factories. *Six Years* sustains the heroic mood. Students read recipes aloud to one another because good food is so scarce. A young Jew knows he is doomed, but his friends rally loyally to his

Still from SOMEWHERE IN HOLLAND

side . . . Thirty years later, Paul Verhoeven's *Soldier of Orange* (see Chapter Seven) disclosed the reality of the situation—the anti-Jewish sentiments, the betrayals, the disunity. At least *Six Years* has the courage to end on a cynical note. "Brave New World," says a young man bitterly, and his words are followed immediately by an image of the nuclear explosion at Bikini.

Ivens (at right) filming BREAKERS

3. JORIS IVENS, THE FLYING DUTCHMAN

Modesty, discretion, artistry, and intelligent observation are the virtues that inform a majority of the short films produced in the Netherlands. Joris Ivens is at once the founder and the opponent of these traditional values. Little wonder that he has remained a father figure to a younger generation of Dutch directors—Weisz, Verstappen, Verhoeven and van der Keuken.

The sobriquet, "Flying Dutchman," is peculiarly appropriate to Joris Ivens. He has made documentaries in eighteen countries and consequently he has lost touch with Holland over the years. He is honoured whenever he returns to Amsterdam, and in 1965-66 he shot *Rotterdam-Europoort,* but his place in Dutch cinema is secured by his work as a pioneer in the late Twenties and early Thirties. Although the Dutch pride themselves on being socially engaged, they recoil from extremes, and Ivens's overtly Communist stand on world issues since the Forties has disconcerted them. The real tragedy of Ivens's career is that while his political commitment has intensified to a zealous degree, his talent as a film-maker has dwindled, so that much of his recent work in Asia appears crude and naïve.

His life, however, has been devoted to film with a single-mindedness one cannot but admire. "Your set is the world," he has written, "and you have to look all around before focusing your camera on a corner of it. Even if you wished to keep aloof, life has a way of making your film a part of it."[4] All Ivens's documentaries have a rough-hewn quality, like newsreels; but they scorn the objectivity of the *genre.* "The newsreel," he emphasises, "tells us *where-when-what;* the documentary film tells us *why,* and the relationship between events."[4] Film is a means to an end for Ivens, a means of presenting truth—truth as he sees it—in a controversial situation, whether it be in Chile or Vietnam, Belgium or China. Throughout his life he has been a witness to circumstances, recording misery and dissension with an uncompromising spirit. The Ivens documentary does not merely inform and touch the spectator; it forces him into a private reaction of his own, rouses in him anger and indignation, against either the film-maker or the events he describes. One may believe that the individual is a more noble creature than the collective, and yet still respond to the passion of Ivens's approach.

He was born on November 18, 1898, in Nijmegen. His father and
grandfather were both involved in the development of photography
in the Netherlands, and Ivens was already making his first film at the
age of thirteen—a Red Indian adventure inspired by Karl May! He
served in the First World War and after the Armistice studied
economics, becoming an active figure in the trade union movement
and campaigning on behalf of Dutch students for better conditions.
He then travelled to Berlin where the inflated mark meant that he
could attend innumerable plays and concerts for next to nothing.
Eager to learn more about the mechanics of photography, he took a
job in Dresden at a camera plant. Here again he was soon voicing the
grievances of the workers. When he returned to Holland in 1926, he
helped to establish the "Filmliga," one of the earliest of film societies
and a tremendous success. He grew friendly with Hendrik Marsman,
among the best Dutch poets of modern times, and with painters and
sculptors who frequented the cafés of Amsterdam. German expres-
sionism was much in vogue at the time, but Ivens, although an
admirer of Ruttmann and Richter, characteristically abandoned all
artificiality when he made his own *début* in 35 mm—an unedited film
about drunks in a bar in the Zeedijk quarter of Amsterdam.

But it was in May 1928 that Ivens really inaugurated the Dutch
cinema, with *The Bridge (De brug),* a study of movement about the
railway drawbridge over the Maas river in Rotterdam. It is the
smoothest of documentaries—a continuous flow of movement and a
tribute to a feat of precision engineering. Ivens creates a visual
symphony of sliding wheels and swinging girders, ending with a train
pouring through the bridge after it has been raised and lowered to
allow a ship to pass beneath. "I learned from *The Bridge*," says Ivens,
"that prolonged and creative observation is the only way to be sure of
selecting, emphasising, and squeezing everything possible out of the
rich reality in front of you."[4] Ivens's work at this time was effected in
close collaboration with Mannus Franken, a writer involved with the
Filmliga. Together they dropped all the traditional baggage of the
film industry—*décor,* studio, acting—and concentrated instead on the
evolution of a realistic documentary style.

Rain (Regen, 1929), perhaps Ivens's most celebrated piece, was
based on a screenplay by Franken,* and reminded Ivens of the lines
by Verlaine:

> *Il pleure dans mon coeur*
> *Comme il pleut sur la ville.*

---

*"Ivens, despairing because of the continual oily autumnal rains—those thick, sober,
well-fed rains of Holland—came to Paris and complained to his friend . . . of nature's
perversity and his own dire condition. 'Well,' said Franken, 'why don't you film the
rain?' " (Harry Alan Potamkin, in *The Compound Cinema,* New York, Teachers College
Press, 1977).

A famous shot from Ivens's RAIN

For four months the minuscule production team photographed shower after shower in order to achieve the desired *look* of wetness. "The rain itself was a moody actress who had to be humoured and who refused anything but natural make-up."[4]

Rain is a dazzling photographic exercise, starting with views of the sunny streets and then noting the wind-troubled canopies above the shops, and the first scattered drops of rain in the canals. As the shower intensifies, the streets themselves look like canals. Everywhere there are rivulets of water, drops that coalesce along the tumbled roofs. The pace of pedestrians caught in the rain increases—at first a mass of confused umbrellas crouching together, then a series of bustling figures hurrying home along the pavements. Thus the basic pattern of an Ivens film is discernible. Movement within the frame is closely tied to the rhythm of the editing; camera movements are not so important. The structure used in *Rain*—situation, incident, return to *status quo ante*—has been followed by Dutch film-makers many times since.

In 1929, Ivens recruited John Fernhout as one of his assistants. Fernhout (later known as Ferno) was only fourteen when he was involved with the production of *Breakers (Branding),* and later he photographed most of Ivens's important work in the Thirties before branching out successfully as a director himself (see Chapter Five).

Breakers tells of an unemployed fisherman who pawns his watch in order to buy a brooch for his *fiancée*. The pawnbroker is a villain like all pawnbrokers, of course, and the youth is tempted to murder him. At the uncertain end, he sails out to sea and the water continues to break and foam over the limitless shore. Ivens and his crew lived in a rented house at Katwijk, a fishing village on the Dutch coast, and constructed an elaborate rubber sack with a glass front that fitted over the camera and Ivens's head and shoulders, so that he could film the sea actually breaking over and around him. The kinetic energy of these shots gives a distinctive lilt and intensity to the film. There is something ineffably touching, too, in the way the sand slides and flows beneath the hands of the young lovers in the dunes. Ironically, *Breakers* is impaired by its awkward performances. Ivens was clearly influenced by the Soviet films of the Twenties, with their large close-ups and heavy, scowling faces.

When Pudovkin was in Amsterdam for a lecture at the Filmliga, he invited Ivens to visit the U.S.S.R., and in December 1929, the Dutchman arrived in Moscow and was at once allowed to stay in Eisenstein's apartment. He travelled to Leningrad, where he met Kozintsev and Trauberg, and on to Kiev, the home of Alexander Dovzhenko, whose *Earth* impressed Ivens deeply. Two years later, he was to return to the Soviet Union and make *Song of Heroes,* a celebration of the burgeoning steel plant at Magnitogorsk.

In 1930, Ivens embarked on the first of his great films about land reclamation. He was the most important chronicler of the Dutch campaign against the sea, a theme that runs like an unbroken thread through Dutch life and culture. It is difficult for the foreigner to grasp the significance of the dikes and windmills to the Dutch. For them, they symbolise not a decorative and picturesque mode of life, but a means of survival, tokens of progress and fortitude. In the words of the poet Roland Holst,

> *"Sometimes I half imagine that the sea*
> *Since powerful it seems, my whole life long will be*
> *The tempestuous reality,*
> *With which I can withstand the world,*
> *Come good, come ill."*

(translated by James Brockway)

Ivens was fascinated by this indigenous source of inspiration. He set out to show how man continually adapts to his environment and to nature's demands. *New Earth* (*Nieuwe gronden,* 1934) is concerned with the construction of an artificial inland sea and the closing of the great barrier dike across the north of the Zuiderzee. This is recorded by Ivens and his three cameras with an ecstatic burst of montage reminiscent of Eisenstein's triumphant sequences at the end of

The procession of workers from NEW EARTH

Battleship Potemkin. Ivens regards the 500 feet (about 125 shots) of this dam-closing sequence as the most complex and successfully dramatic editing he has ever done. Hanns Eisler's music is wedged humorously against the images, giving an almost choreographic effect to the shots of men tossing stones and carrying pipes in unison.

The Thirties were a crucial period in Ivens's development. He gradually shuffled off the aesthetic style that had marked *The Bridge, Rain* and *Breakers,* in favour of a sharper, more purposeful form of cinema. For Ivens, it is the organisation of shots, of "raw material," that is vital if the truth is to be presented in a dynamic, provocative way. The most bitter part of *New Earth* is the last reel, when one sees the harvest, grown on hard-won land, being thrown back into the sea because of the depression of 1930.

Borinage (1933), made in Belgium, brings into focus the struggle between the miners at Borinage and the authorities, and Ivens's grave, objective camera conveys the workers' grim determination to prevail as they trudge through the streets on the Fiftieth Anniversary of Karl Marx's death. Shots of families camping in tiny rooms, or scraping worthless coal from the tips in an attempt to keep warm, still carry the feel of a crisis, even if they were staged and fabricated by Ivens to suit his cause. "Every sequence should say I ACCUSE," maintains Ivens, "accusing the social system which caused such misery and hardship . . . Our aim was to prevent agreeable photographic effects distracting the audience from the unpleasant truths we were showing."[4] One is reminded strongly of Barbara Kopple and her documentary on the Kentucky miners' strike of 1973, in *Harlan County U.S.A.*

Spanish Earth, filmed at the height of the Civil War in 1937, is given immense weight by Ernest Hemingway's commentary. His impassioned description of this battle between the "will of the military" and the "will of the people" is an ideal counterpoint to the images— images seized with courage and sensitivity from the most dangerous quarters of the war by Ivens and Fernhout. The predominant impression is of a pastoral people coming to terms with fighting: tanks are incongruous in the placid fields; after work the peasants drill together. But the intermittent massacres bring home the more nightmarish aspects of the Civil War: doomed figures dashing across the street as shells scream down on a summer's afternoon. Though its visuals comprise an ugly mosaic of conflict and destruction, *Spanish Earth* is still an idealistic film, expressing an unshakable faith in "the clenched fists of republican Spain."

Ivens then visited China, where he made *The 400 Million,* dealing with the Chinese response to the Japanese invasion, recording the panic of dispossessed men, women and children as they flee beleaguered cities. (The camera Ivens gave to the Chinese when he departed now rests in a Peking museum.) Next, the U.S.A., where he undertook *The Power and the Land* for the U.S. Film Service; and

Street scene from SPANISH EARTH

Canada, where at the invitation of John Grierson he shot *Action Stations,* about the Canadian naval effort in the war. Although he discussed projects with Wellman and Pozner, Ivens did not make a feature film during his stay in America, and in 1945 he went to Australia and assembled *Indonesia Calling.* The Indonesians were still fighting for their independence at this stage, for the Dutch wanted to return, according to the commentary, to their "treasure islands." The film centres on the Australian dockers' and sailors' refusal to handle Dutch ships that were intended "to break the back of the young republic," and there are effective moments when, for example, a picket vessel harangues a military ship with an interpreter translating urgently through a megaphone and the soldiers booing in return.

This powerful left-wing propaganda ingratiated Ivens with the Communist bloc, just as it mortified the Dutch authorities, who had already been shocked when Ivens resigned as Film Commissioner for the Netherlands East Indies government in protest against the "undemocratic" attitude of his employers. He was invited to Czechoslovakia, Poland, and the young German Democratic Republic. Some of Ivens's best postwar films, like *The Song of the Rivers* (*Lied der Ströme,* 1954), have been made in Eastern Europe, although *La Seine a rencontré Paris* strongly revives the romantic vision of his youth, with a commentary by Jacques Prévert that imparts a lyrical flow to the journey by barge up the Seine. *Song of the Rivers,* by contrast, brings together workers from various countries, stressing their mutual desire to combat oppression, and using six of the world's principal rivers as a unifying *motif.*

Ivens has worked ceaselessly these past years. In Italy he shot a television feature about the ugly disparities in the national economy (the film was, accordingly, heavily cut); in Cuba, where he gave lessons at the national film institute (ICAIC), he was responsible for two shorts about the independence campaign; and in Chile he collaborated with Chris Marker on *A Valparaiso,* one of his finest documentaries. Marker's words, like Hemingway's in *Spanish Earth,* bring a dignity and a muted anguish to the picture of a city cramped almost to death against the hills, a city once a major port of call—before the Panama Canal was opened.

Ivens returned to the Netherlands in 1965 to shoot his first film there for several years—*Rotterdam-Europoort.* It was a sympathetic glance, in colour, at the people who make possible the prestige of the city of Rotterdam, but it tried to assimilate too many individual elements (an amateur performance of "The Flying Dutchman," burning buildings during the war) for it to have the satisfying cadence of Ivens's vintage films. It is characteristic of his involvement in man's struggles against invasion that in the past decade he has spent much time in South-East Asia, producing such films as *The Threatening Sky* (*Le 17ème parallele,* 1968), a trenchant account of the Vietnamese response and resistance to American bombing, and *Le peuple et ses fusils* (1969) about the conflict in Laos. He contributed a segment to the portmanteau production, *Loin du Viêtnam* (1967), in which he extols the civil defence that Hanoi marshalled so successfully against American bombing. Again, the argument is simplistic and one-sided, but the report has a pictorial naturalism worthy of the best Ivens. Would he, one wonders, ever make—or be permitted to make—a film about present day Ho Chi Minh City (Saigon) and the agony of those forced into the countryside or held in detention centres for "re-education"?

Ivens has during the Seventies completed an enormous fresco of contemporary China, under the title *How Yukong Moved the Mountains.* Its twelve episodes run to more than eleven hours, and they have been screened widely on television. A typical section describes the daily routine and fledgling technology of the oilfields in the northern province of Taking. The underlying theme of the whole film is the Cultural Revolution and its impact on life in China. As always in Ivens, the emphasis is on people rather than places; the vast cities and plains of China are insignificant by comparison with shopkeepers, technicians, teachers, and peasants. Ivens admits that when he strolled round Dutch museums in his youth, "Nature meant little more than a setting for human activity. Even Brueghel's landscapes were to me just backgrounds for the living, moving, dancing people in the foreground."[4] One must praise Ivens's courage in switching his allegiance from an orthodox admiration for Soviet society to an open-minded appreciation of Chinese life, a pattern of existence much frowned upon by Moscow. But he had been friendly for years with prominent figures such as Chou-en-lai, and had been much impressed by the country when he made *The 400 Million* in 1938. It was Chou who suggested in 1971 that Ivens and Marcelle Loridan bring their cameras to China again, to confront a country that had moved from feudalism to a communistic democracy in less than a generation. Perhaps this perennially young-in-spirit *cinéaste* is drawn instinctively to the early phase in a people's fight for liberation; had he been in Russia sixty years ago, he would have been using film to help the Bolshevik Revolution, so it is only natural that today, in his declining years, he should gravitate towards China, where time has not yet brought corruption and cynicism in its train.

4. BERT HAANSTRA - HUMANIST AND HUMORIST

If Joris Ivens is the greatest name in Dutch cinema prior to the Second World War, there is no doubt that Bert Haanstra is the most brilliant figure to have emerged in the postwar period. Like Ivens, he is a documentarist *par excellence,* but the two men are poles apart in attitude. Ivens seeks to change society into more idealistic patterns, while Haanstra observes and analyses folk as they are, caught up fleetingly in the human comedy. For Ivens, there is injustice in the plight of so many people; for Haanstra, there is rather a natural order of things, and if even once in a lifetime one contrives to reach one's neighbour through laughter or tragedy, one has justified one's existence. Ivens is the polemicist, Haanstra the *raconteur.* Ivens was fascinated by film technique for only a brief period at the beginning of his career; the art of montage, however, is a significant ally in Haanstra's quest for man's soul (e.g. the dissolves blending those self-portraits at the close of *Rembrandt, Painter of Men*). Yet, ultimately and profoundly, both men are linked by their affection for humanity.

Haanstra's father and his two brothers were painters, and he himself has executed posters and portraits professionally during his life. From the age of twelve he longed to make films, his enthusiasm fired by a local projectionist in Goor who allowed him to watch programmes through the cabin window. "My parents wanted me to see Chaplin and Lloyd and no one else. But I loved others too, especially a couple of zany Danish comedians." Haanstra built his own projector, and his first camera was a 9.5mm, hand-cranked machine; he used it to make a number of amateur films. He took up a career as a press photographer and was at the Academy of Arts during the war. There he met a German refugee, Paul Bruno Schreiber, who gave him the chance to be cameraman on a feature film then being planned. This saw the light in 1948, as the fantasy, *Myrthe en de demonen,* but during its creation Haanstra's life and ambitions had completely changed. He came to England and devoted nine months to the sound recording and editing of Schreiber's feature. Excited by the resources of Denham—and then by lavish praise for his photography on the otherwise disastrous picture—he resolved to be a film-maker.

Haanstra's first independent short, *De Muiderkring herleeft* (1949)

Left: undulating buildings in MIRROR OF HOLLAND. Right: PANTA RHEI

reveals, in retrospect, many of the ideas and the technical skill that mark his subsequent work. It was made by Haanstra from start to finish—literally. He borrowed money to buy a second-hand camera, and received only six hundred florins for his eight months of work on the film. He even drew the credits, while his wife made the costumes. The subject was unusual. The castle of Muiden had been a cultural rendezvous in the Seventeenth century, and a well-known modern Dutch poet used to revive the spirit of Muiden by presiding over cultural "Circles" regularly there. Haanstra's film is a reconstruction of the original gatherings: poems by Vondel and P.C. Hooft are recited to the accompaniment of the harpsichord. It is only apprentice work, but it is rich in moments of thoughtful observation and wry humour, and the underlying theme—the continuity of life in the face of physical change and decay—is one to which Dutch directors have resorted increasingly since.

Mirror of Holland (Spiegel van Holland), which won the Grand Prix for Shorts at Cannes in 1951, and first established Haanstra's name abroad, is based on a supremely original notion: the life of the Netherlands as reflected in the canals that lace the country. Stately buildings undulate and lose their dignity, the sails of yachts wriggle comically. Gradually the insubstantial shapes take on an abstract life of their own—everything is in motion—and the absence of a commentary (rare at that period) seems a positive advantage. "I was staggered by the applause at Cannes," recalls Haanstra. "I'd had no subsidy for *Mirror of Holland,* but after the festival I sold the world rights to the Ministry of Arts, and I felt that my future really lay in film-making."

This translucent quality and the conception of *perpetuum mobile* reappear even more seriously in *Panta rhei* (1951), a cinematic demonstration of Heracleitus's axiom that all things flow. But Haanstra does not share the Ephesian's melancholy stance. For him the axiom is a means of extolling nature and of showing the sensuous undercurrent of life itself. Even in his feature films, Haanstra is searching for that indefinable mechanism that animates not merely the sea and the sky but the human race as well. The visual power of *Panta rhei* is extraordinary. The water, as in most of Haanstra's work, is the source from which all things draw life. Clusters of clouds billow swiftly like smoke or steam; flocks of birds wheel like black dust flung in arcs throughout the sky; the sun's reflection shimmers in a thousand points of light on the surface of the sea. The masterly editing and the inventive use of slow- and fast-motion raise the film to the level of an ode to nature.

Medieval Dutch Sculpture (*Nederlandse beeldhouwkunst tijdens de late middeleeuwen*, 1951), made just beforehand, is not a favourite of Haanstra's, despite the fluidity of the style and the devotion to the subject. He has never been stimulated by the "art film" as such, and it is amazing that he should have succeeded so well with *Rembrandt* in 1956. Before that, Haanstra worked under Sir Arthur Elton and the Shell Film Unit. He now recognises it as one of the most valuable periods of his career. At one stage he shot four films in five months in Indonesia, without scripts, and could not even see the rushes. But these four shorts proved to be models of lucid instruction, and are screened repeatedly to students of oil and to scientific audiences. Most important of all, they prepared Haanstra for the complicated rigours of *The Rival World* (1954), a documentary commissioned by Shell, about man's fight to control insects, that ranks among the finest and most dynamic of its type to be produced since the war. Haanstra was working in colour for the first time and used it to fierce effect: the close-ups of the locusts are terrifying and yet strangely beautiful.

Haanstra's three documentaries about the sea (*The Dike Builders, And There Was No More Sea . . ., Delta Phase One*) are all admirably made and illustrate the director's preoccupation with that unique love-hate relationship with the water on which Dutch life is founded. *And There Was No More Sea . . .* (*En de zee was niet meer . . .*, 1956), edited with wit and compassion, describes the end of an era for the Amsterdamer as the Ijssel Meer is closed by a massive dike. Haanstra emphasises the traditions that will die hard—the laying out of nets, the eel lines being hauled in (one of the director's most fluent sequences), and the Sunday worship for fisherfolk. Haanstra *is* a traditionalist; time for him weathers a public habit into virtue, softens its outlines to a quaint and charming spectacle.

But others have made equally good films on the same theme. Haanstra's talent lies in different quarters. Who can deny the power of impeccable technique to achieve moments of sheer poetry after seeing the closing minutes of *Rembrandt, Painter of Men?* A series of dissolves from one self-portrait to another registers the essence of the artist's entire life and development in terms that are triumphantly,

Haanstra and his crew filming "The Night Watch" for REMBRANDT, PAINTER OF MEN

purely cinematic. Concentrating on about sixty paintings, Haanstra relates the events in Rembrandt's life to his work. The tragic death of his children, his fear for Titus's health, the ingratitude of the burghers—all seem mirrored in the spiritual troubles that weigh on Rembrandt's Biblical figures and on his own head in the self-portraits. Haanstra's respectful treatment, epitomised in the advancement and withdrawal of the camera, succeeds in conveying that refulgent, three-dimensional quality in Rembrandt's art. The film was made for the 350th anniversary of the artist's birth.

But the apotheosis of Haanstra's documentary career was yet to come. In 1957 the Royal Leerdam Glass Works commissioned him to make an instructional film about the manufacture of glass. Haanstra agreed, but only on condition that he be allowed to make a second, shorter film on glass for his own amusement. "I was fascinated," he recalls, "by the robot-like nature of the machines." Ironically enough, it is Haanstra's own little fantasy, *Glass (Glas),* that has now become a legend among film societies all over the world. By 1963 a thousand prints were in circulation. Haanstra's warm, humorous approach to his subject is the key to the film's appeal, and the climax comes when a mechanical stacking machine goes wrong because of a single bottle. It is the *total* impression of *Glass* that lingers: a robust symphony of processes that describes practically every stage in the making of glass objects. The rhythm of the editing matches perfectly the rhythm

Still from Haanstra's documentary, GLASS

within the frame. *Glass* won an Academy Award in 1960, and major prizes at more than a dozen festivals.

One senses that Haanstra is by instinct a short film specialist. Only in recent years have his features commanded as much respect as his documentaries. *Fanfare* (1958) enjoyed immense commercial success

Recalcitrant beast in Haanstra's bucolic comedy, FANFARE

in Holland. It is a tale of faction fighting among rival groups trying to dominate a village brass band, and Haanstra employs the bucolic background to droll effect. In some ways, *Fanfare* is reminiscent of the vintage Ealing comedies (and Alexander Mackendrick helped on the script), but there are typical Haanstra touches too, such as the witty comparison of ducks and cattle with the pomposity of the village characters. Gags are blithely timed: a clandestine rehearsal in the barn is ruined by startled hens, who flutter into the horns and tubas; a cow prances impetuously through a ladies' tea party, scattering guests in flight. Like all good Ealing movies, *Fanfare* ends in a resolution of conflict, a unity of rivals, as the two bands—side by side on the competition platform—discover that their melodies blend together in a totally unforeseen, and winning, orchestration. This choice of *peripeteia* is inspired, for it draws on visual and musical resources, and harks back to the band's very first rehearsals in the village hall. Such compactness of scripting has not often been achieved in Holland, and compels one to admit that the best Dutch films, like *Fanfare* and *Max Havelaar,* are not so much international as *national* in texture and quality.

Despite the profitability of his first feature, Haanstra encountered difficulty in financing a second fiction film. He wrote the original screenplay of *The Silent Raid* (*De overval*, a wartime story later filmed with some competence by Paul Rotha), at a period when war subjects were somewhat risky in a Dutch context. Finally he decided to produce a film himself. The result was *The M.P. Case* (*De zaak M.P.*, 1960), the most disastrous and expensive failure in Haanstra's career. The plot revolves round the *risqué* statuette in Brussels known as the "Manneke Pis," and the contention between groups of Dutch and Belgian students after the annual soccer match between the two countries (Haanstra has always been mad on football). It transpires that a university worker has stolen the statue in order to become a hero by finding it again. More professionally executed than *Fanfare, The M.P. Case* is artificial in construction.

Since then, Haanstra has more than recovered both his critical reputation and his financial losses. He turned, with rewarding results, to the "candid camera" technique. *Zoo* (1962) is a diverting little exercise in which, Haanstra says, he has "tried to see the zoo as a very pleasant and interesting places where watching people is quite as interesting as watching animals." A girl's striped dress resembles a zebra; a woman eating a huge sandwich is uncomfortably close to a lioness gnawing her midday meat. It was, incidentally, greatly admired by Jacques Tati, who bought it for his own distribution company and insisted that it be played with his own features in French cinemas. Tati and Haanstra have become fast friends over the years, and in the early Seventies Haanstra contributed some excellent ideas to the Amsterdam sequences of *Traffic*. His son, Rimko Haanstra, was also launched in France through Tati, who responded to the sprightly

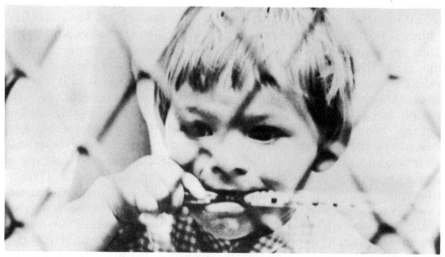

Boy behind bars in ZOO

Still from THE HUMAN DUTCH

animation of *Black and White* (1971) and the slow-burning comedy of *One in a Thousand (Duizend zielen,* 1976).

Haanstra's *The Human Dutch (Alleman,* 1963) is a masterpiece of its kind. Superficially a documentary about the Dutch, it comes as near as any film can to catching the underlying rhythm of a nations's life. At certain moments, too, it has a significance far beyond the parochial habits it portrays. Haanstra observes his fellow creatures with tolerance and a gentle wit. The candid camera shots are never exploited maliciously, and Haanstra regards the technique as the only truly effective means of recording people as they behave naturally. "It's so easy to shock," he admits, "but I wanted to make a picture that showed people not as dogs, in the Jacopetti sense, but as recognisable human beings." The scenes of bargaining in the cattle-markets, the masked ball where appearances distort emotions, the shyness of fresh arrivals at a school, all transcend their immediate context and become a commentary on mankind in general. Running through *The Human Dutch* like a fugue is a profound, vigorous respect for man—for his capacity to be sad, jovial, individualistic, religious, self-sufficient, and above all *free* (expressed in that deftest of shots: the skater swooping gracefully along a canal without a soul in sight). Who could equal the dexterity of such moments as the uncanny dissolves that compare places now to what they were in wartime, or the dispirited band that shuffles along in the rain? These evince the poet in Haanstra, just as the soundtrack, lavish with spoken puns, betrays in him the humorist.

The Voice of the Water (De stem van het water, 1966) has the contours of a travelogue, but Haanstra, like the boats on a crowded river, weaves his way past the usual *clichés.* He glances wryly at the tourist's traditional image of Holland and in his commentary he underlines the paradoxical facts of Dutch life—most ground below sea level and, "Other nations pray for rain, but Holland has too much water." He chuckles visually at the Dutch craze for owning boats (one shot shows a wife and daughter scrubbing the side of a cruiser while the husband reads his paper on board); he draws surprising wit from the arrival of Saint Nicholas, to the acclaim of children everywhere; and he makes generous fun of a little boy's reluctance to swim.

But there is an obverse to Haanstra's humour, and this inspires the film's finest sequences. There is, for instance, Klaas Buitenhuis, the eel fisherman who rises before dawn to inspect his nets and offers some passionate and percipient remarks on his way of life and his sense of "a higher Power"—Nature, God, or Whatever—as he glides like Charon over the misty waters, the silence disturbed only by the creak of the rowlock. Or those poignant shots of old folk discussing suicide and the fear of death in the water. Or the Brueghel-like compositions as children skate and play on an icy pond with the huge Dutch sky about them. Or the 1953 disaster, when more than 1,800 people perished in floods, and a bereaved mother reads once more

The fisherman at dawn, in THE VOICE OF THE WATER

her letter describing the catastrophe, the camera panning round to
discover her on a breakwater with her only surviving son, both their
faces grave and stoical. So Haanstra lends plastic immediacy to
Marshman's poem:

> . . . and far and wide
> the voice of the water,
> of endless disaster
> Is feared and heard.

Far from humiliating people by his observations, Haanstra
ennobles them, and in *Ape and Super-Ape* (*Bij de beesten af,* 1973) he
emphasises that man has the chance and the ability to interpret his
past and his relationship with the animal world. He begins mischie-
vously by quoting the English bishop's wife who, on hearing it
announced that man was descended from the apes, exclaimed, "Let
us hope that it is not true, but if it is, let us pray that it doesn't become
generally known." This feature-length documentary absorbed three,
dedicated years of Haanstra's life and, while it draws on the research
conducted by such eminent authorities as Konrad Lorenz and G.P.
Baerends, it is unmistakably the product of the mind that created
Panta rhei, Glass, Zoo, and *The Human Dutch.* Haanstra, using locations
in Africa, Antarctica, North and South America, India, and Europe,
studies a vast range of animals in their natural habitat, and distin-
guishes their behavioural patterns—their aggression, their territorial
jealousy, their hierarchical responses, their mating habits—in a series
of close-up encounters that have seldom been surpassed on film (the
penguin sequence is outstanding). Often the parallels with human
gestures and actions are patently clear. Haanstra, however, even in

The chimpanzees from the Gombe Valley, in APE AND SUPER-APE

the final part of *Ape and Super-Ape,* never accentuates the resemblances too didactically, never searches for an easy laugh at the expense of a particular species. The qualities in nature that inspire Haanstra—its freedom from those ideologies and theories so seductive to man, its lack of sentimentality—are, finally, the qualities that attract one to his own keenly-tempered films.

Haanstra deplores the absence of any tradition of drama, let alone screenwriting, in Dutch culture. "It's so hard to find a good *story,*" he complains. But *When the Poppies Bloom Again (Dokter Pulder zaait papavers,* 1975) is derived from a true incident, on which Anton Koolhaas based a novel. Koolhaas is an old friend of Haanstra's, and in 1974 spent his holidays in a hotel in Laren writing the screenplay like a man possessed. The resulting film is quite unlike anything Haanstra has ever done. There is a dark, Satanic figure in this particular carpet, and the ingrown pattern of village life is recorded with a gravity and precision worthy of Dreyer. Dr. Pulder is a sane, rational family doctor whose routine is disturbed by a visitor from the past, Hans van Inge Liedaerd, a neuro-surgeon who studied at university with him. By degrees, Hans crumbles. Throughout the evening's reunion, he veers alarmingly from genial assertiveness to inscrutable melancholy. He falls drunk, and steals morphine from Pulder's locked dispensary, leaving the key derisively in a bowl of urine. He vanishes, and soon succumbs to his addiction.

Haanstra and Koolhaas divide the film into two distinct halves. In the first part, Pulder acquits himself with courtesy and credit. He is puzzled by Hans's admiration for him, but keeps his visitor at bay with a tolerant wit. The moment he learns of Hans's death, however, he undergoes a subtle sea-change. Hans's lifestyle begins to exert, in retrospect as it were, a curious appeal; his friend, Pulder realises, was searching for a more challenging dimension to his existence. His wife warns him that he is trying, even if unconsciously, to imitate Hans. But Pulder, impetuous, plunges on. He becomes friends with a mistress of Hans, Mrs. Mies (brilliantly created by the Belgian actress, Dora van der Groen), whose memories of her former lover reveal him in an increasingly bizarre light. Pulder finds himself seduced, more psychologically than physically, by this drunken bag of a woman. Together they sow poppies in her back garden, a macabre ballet for two deranged and deluded human beings. Pulder is eventually brought to his senses by a road accident and by the suicide of Mrs. Mies; only then is he free of the spell cast by Hans. As Kees Fens has pointed out, in Koolhaas's writings, "the urge to live leads to death, and mortality is disguised as vitality."[1]

For a film so full of dialogue, *When the Poppies Bloom Again* is unusually tense and disquieting. Hitchcock and Chabrol would smile at the early scene when Pulder cuts his finger while preparing snacks for his visitor, and blood dribbles on to the fresh cubes of cheese. It is a

Kees Brusse and Henny Orri in WHEN THE POPPIES BLOOM AGAIN

neat (and amusing) symbol of the danger that lies just beyond the fringe of mundane experience. The entire sequence in Pulder's house when the friends have returned tipsy from dinner, and each in his room frets and talks to himself, is controlled by Haanstra with an absolute rigour and assurance. The absurd joins forces with the tragic throughout this movie; even the much-criticised episode in a hotel where Hans falls asleep with his basin tap running, and the restaurant below is flooded, is perfectly justified in context; farce it may be, but farce filtered through the inebriated memory of Mrs. Mies.

When the Poppies Bloom Again could so easily have been cynical in tone. But Haanstra obviously sympathises with Pulder in his efforts to explore a region of the mind hitherto untapped. Each of us makes in his life at least one such attempt to flee the everyday. Pulder's escapade nearly wrecks his social standing, but it also brings forth qualities—tolerance, warmth of feeling, even passion—that a professional career has quietly buried.

Just as Haanstra anthropomorphises the beasts and birds of his documentary films, so in his dramatic work he unveils the natural urges and instincts man is heir to. He does so, however, with compassion rather than irony; in him, the humanist inevitably prevails.

5. THE DOCUMENTARY TRADITION

Sponsorship in the Netherlands is an age-old tradition, from which even Rembrandt derived some kind of livelihood. Although that very term, sponsorship, implies a degree of control over the artist, the situation in Holland is surprisingly tolerant. Joris Ivens, for example, was allowed by Philips to make *Industrial Symphony,* one of his first critical analyses of capitalist methods.

Film sponsors are of various shapes and sizes: from the Ministry of Culture, Recreation and Social Welfare to Royal Dutch Shell, from the airline KLM to the Netherlands Foreign Office. It is usually the government to which the aspiring young film-maker will turn. If his script is approved by the Ministry of Culture (which acts on advice given it by the Film Department of the Arts Council), the budget will often be met in full, in the form of a non-punitive grant, and yet the director's artistic control will not be threatened. This can lead to a limitation of outlook and approach, but there is no denying the range of themes—fiction and non-fiction—that lie open to the "sponsored directors" of the Netherlands: biographies and profiles, war stories, comedies, surrealist fantasies, topographical studies. State aid for the cinema is, after all, a matter of degree, and the attitude of the Ministry of Culture in The Hague is by ordinary standards extremely versatile.

In recent years, a budding director in Holland has seen his horizon of opportunity broadened with the growth of alternative organisations such as Fugitive Cinema, and the now-defunct STOFF (Studio for Developing Film and Film Manifestations); the determination of independent producers like Nico Crama, Jan Vrijman, and Rolf Orthel to produce shorts; and the startling commitment displayed by TV stations such as VPRO (see Chapter Ten). Television generally in the Netherlands gives the film world some positive help by screening more and more Dutch shorts, which might otherwise never reach the local population.

A majority of the shorts completed in Holland are sold to world markets through the RVD (Netherlands Information Service), which has a full-time sales force and arranges promotion and distribution of short films at home and abroad.

The documentary tradition in the Netherlands has both profited from, and survived, such official beneficence. There have been scores of competent directors in the postwar period, and it would be impossible to discuss all of them or all of their films in the context of this book. Haanstra, to whom an entire chapter is devoted, is clearly the pivotal figure, followed closely by Herman van der Horst, Charles Huguenot van der Linden, and John Ferno. Hattum Hoving, Jan Vrijman, and Theo van Haren Noman are also included in this section, but I have given space in Chapter Eight to maverick talents such as Johan van der Keuken, Louis van Gasteren, and George Sluizer.

A. CHARLES HUGUENOT VAN DER LINDEN

Charles Huguenot van der Linden, now in his sixties, has always strained against the bit of both the short and the documentary idiom. His prewar feature, *Young Hearts* (see Chapter Two), is far removed from the sobriety of the typical Dutch documentary. Van der Linden is the perennial non-conformist, even if he does still live today in the house where he was born, in Amsterdam's elegant P.C. Hoofstraat. "I've always been ahead of my time," he says. "People are afraid of too much violence, and censorship problems. It's an uphill battle to secure finance for an unusual film in Holland. Nowadays the big sponsors spend their money on TV commercials."

The head of Paramount in the Netherlands visited the school where van der Linden was President of the drama circle, and selected him for a post in the American company. He trained as an editor, preparing Dutch versions of films from the United States. He also edited Paramount's *Eyes and Ears of the World* for local consumption, and spent many interesting days in Berlin on assignment for the newsreel. It was a splendid education. Each evening he would see the latest films, and next morning had to report on them to his superiors at Paramount. One of his assistants there was H.M. Josephson, later a director in his own right. "Before the war there was no continuity in the Dutch cinema," recalls van der Linden. "Second raters were brought over from Germany to prop up the industry. You could never teach a crew to achieve better and better results. Rudy Meyer was really the only—and the best—producer we ever had."

Van der Linden, perhaps the most audacious of all the Dutch film-makers despite his self-effacing charm, has contributed enormously to the growth of that "tradition" of technical excellence and conciseness of expression so characteristic of postwar Dutch cinema. There are the skilful, straightforward accounts of national life and incidents, such as *Back to the Island* (*Terug naar het eiland,* 1950), about the liberation of Walcheren, *Deep Holland* (*Diep Neder-land,* 1956), about drilling for oil, and *Skilled Hands Ready* (*Vakman paraat*), about industrial training. *Dutch in Seven Lessons* (1948) was a semi-documentary made for J. Arthur Rank, who during the im-mediate postwar period could not transfer his company's earnings back to England. Audrey Hepburn applied for the main part, came to see van der Linden, who was moving house at the time, sat on a packing crate and immediately charmed him. She made her *début* in *Dutch in Seven Lessons,* and van der Linden wanted to give her a role in a feature film; but finance was not forthcoming, and soon Ms. Hepburn moved to England, and then to Hollywood.

Two of van der Linden's most exciting shorts are *Interlude by Candlelight (Tussenspel bij Kaarslicht,* 1959), and *Big City Blues* (1962). Both have a disturbing, almost sinister dimension: Harry van Tusschenbroek's puppets, made from bird's skeletons and other refuse, combed from the shoreline by the old gentleman, come to eerie life after dark in *Interlude by Candlelight;* and *Big City Blues,* with its stark, formal story of attempted rape, and death, shows that van der Linden is capable like Stan Brakhage of manipulating sound, image, and situation to create a study in fear that has connotations far beyond the boy-and-girl context in which it is set. The faults in both pieces are faults of execution (hammy acting in the fiction featurette, melodramatic climaxes) rather than of conception. *Big City Blues,* staged in a half-finished building, is as much in key with the inscrutable advances of our scientific age as are parts of *L'eclisse.* This

Still from INTERLUDE BY CANDLELIGHT

Pursuit in the building site, from BIG CITY BLUES

is not to suggest a detailed comparison between van der Linden and Antonioni, but simply to stress that not all Dutch films are oblivious of changes in man's outlook and anxieties. The grainy photography, the geometric patterns of the building, the harsh, unrelated noises on the soundtrack, generate an atmosphere that is weird and dreamlike, shattered by the brutal realism of its climax as the girl is killed by her drunken pursuer. The film was nominated for an Academy Award.

Big City Blues was made on location, which in itself was unusual for a fiction film at that period in the Netherlands. Theatre owners and distributors felt that van der Linden was absurd in trying to expand this theme of violence into a full-length feature, *The Wild Years,* which was to have been a dramatic inquiry into the motives behind the kleptomania of a group of juvenile delinquents. *Or Don't You Dare?* (*. . . Of durf je niet?,* 1965) follows a similar theme with its dramatic interpretation of the teenage sexual experience. Despite censorship problems in a morally conscious country, van der Linden has always been concerned with human distortions and the relationship between the sexes. "Goodness is a negative quality," he once told me, with a smile.

Van der Linden is also a man of wit and compassion. The first quality is illustrated in *The Building Game* (*Bouwspelement,* 1963), which won a Golden Bear at Berlin, the second emerges in *View of Middelharnis* (*Het zwarte zand,* 1954), a documentary on the consequences of the flood disaster that struck the Netherlands in 1953. His career was crowned in 1973 when he finally won an Oscar in Hollywood for *This Tiny World* (*Die kleine wereld*), a charming tribute to the toys that lie abandoned in a Dutch museum. Before the camera, they come to life. "Perhaps it is the passing years that give our toys a soul," says the commentary, as dolls, ships, cars, trains, and aircraft parade with grace and style on the eternal tabletop.

One of this director's most fetching shorts is *The Morning Star* (*De morgenster*, 1957). It is dawn, and a shabby young woman scrounges the streets and canals for scraps. If she finds a sodden shawl, she wrings it out gladly and pops it into the sack she carries over her shoulder. She finds a feather boa here, a statuette there. She stares longingly into a dressmaker's window; she tries on a cheeky hat. Suddenly she puts on a pair of glasses that convert her grey world into a riot of colour; when they break, the film returns to monochrome, and the poor rag-picker's illusions are lost. Finally, she rejoins her husband, a junk dealer who looks dispassionately at her haul.

Van de Linden's camera is adventurous and perky, always keeping out of sight, so to speak, and discovering the decrepit urban landscape as though for the first time. By inserting moments of joy, beauty, and amusement, he makes the prevailing gloom bearable, even salutary. There is more cinematic skill in this apparently coarsely-woven film than in a dozen orthodox docmentaries; there is poetry, too, and the stirring of romance.

Indefatigable, van der Linden is working today on a feature film script, entitled, provisionally, *The Seven Ages of Man*. His wife,

The young woman who roams the streets in THE MORNING STAR

Martina, has acted as producer and helpmate on all his films. Van der Linden is unique in his enormous span of activity in the Dutch film field, for he has been on the scene for half a century, and has adapted to each new phase without compromising his own quirkish vision of life.

B. HERMAN VAN DER HORST

The death of Herman van der Horst a few years ago was a severe loss to the Dutch cinema. Many regarded this dedicated and painstaking director, who lived like a recluse in the tiny village of Vogelenzang, as the best documentarist in Holland. Certainly no one has rendered nature films so relevant as did van der Horst; every sigh of wind, every curlew's call, every wave's roar, is an eloquent proclamation in his work. For van der Horst the soundtrack was as crucial (and never more so than in his colourful study of Surinam, *Faja Lobbi*) as the montage, and in his films the images and natural noises form a delicate syncopation. He was never satisfied unless he was able to control every aspect of his productions from start to finish, and admitted to me that he knew of no country outside the Netherlands where he could obtain such independence. His films were long in gestation, chiefly on account of his meticulous attention to detail. He cared little for the wider world of the cinema (although in his youth he was impressed by *Trader Horn*). Van der Horst was a naturalist at

Still from Herman van der Horst's SHOOT THE NETS

heart, but he had a poet's eye and ear, and would never be satisfied with the straightforward sponsored documentary.

His first effort, *Metamorphosis (Metamorphose)* was screened at the Cannes Festival in 1945, and revealed his fascination with biology. His photographic talent was further confirmed by *Tarnished Land (Ontluisterd land)* and the whimsical *Along Untrodden Dunes (Langs ongebaende klingen,* 1951).

Three documentaries on fishing and the sea established van der Horst's reputation in Dutch cinema during the Fifties, and indeed as a successor to Grierson. *Shoot the Nets (Het schot is te boord)* was a paean to the herring fishermen who plied the cold North Sea; *Lekko* was a vivid impression of a trawler's routine at sea; and *Praise the Sea* brought together in splendid resonance the bells and windmills and water wheels of Holland, a nation dependent on water and married eternally to its dynamic spirit. By now it was clear that van der Horst was a master of the film symphony, and in *Steady! (Houen zo)* he orchestrated the sights and sounds of Rotterdam as it recovered from the wounds of war. Boys play among the ruins as primitive machinery constructs a future from the wreckage. . . The port maintains its urgent round. The chants of the fish market are unceasing. Van der Horst captures with bewildering ease the rhythm and fluency of people involved in physical work. He does not impose an artificial

Still from Herman van der Horst's PAN

Above: Herman van der Horst directing FAJA LOBBI

Above: the organist playing in the final minutes of TOCCATA

structure on the film; instead he seems to *detect*, and then to emphasise, a pulse concealed from average eyes.

This fragile, gossamer gift was always threatened by a story. In *Pan* (1962), for instance, the atmosphere of the reed country is superbly evoked, but the notion of a boy whose intrusion into Nature's realm unleashes the fury of a swan is rather coy and artificial. *Toccata* (1968), his last film, absorbs just a dash of narrative into its blend of music and architectural imagery. A small boy searches for his cat in the Old Church in Amsterdam, while an organist practises Bach on his great Eighteenth-century instrument, struggling at first against a cacophony of workmen's hammering, jets' screaming overhead, and a cleaner's hoovering the floor. The rhythm accelerates almost imperceptibly until in the final few minutes the organist flings heart and soul into Bach's Toccata in F, with the physical effort of manipulating the baroque organ counterpointed by his shouts and exclamations to his assistants, and by the climbing beauty of the music itself.

The danger that attends the solitary film-maker is that he may fail to sense when to trim his work. Van der Horst was at his most imposing in his short films. *Faja Lobbi* (1959), although it dazzled one with its colours, ran for over an hour, and was too impressionistic to sustain one's full attention. The camera explores the forest depths of Surinam, gradually returning to the modern city of Paramaribo, where the film concludes in a raucous, imaginatively composed tour

The great bell of the Great Church in Amsterdam lours over the city in Herman van der Horst's documentary, AMSTERDAM

of the squares and markets, where different races and cultures, religions and traditions, meet in a chromatic collision.

In 1965, van der Horst was a member of the Short Film Jury in Cannes, and at the same festival his own work, *Amsterdam,* was screened. This documentary succeeds in matching the spirit of the Seventeenth century, its burghers and rose-tinted women gazing from Old Master paintings, with the more shrill, vibrant activity of the city today. Yet for van der Horst, the serenity and the innocence can still be found in the statues and the canals, and in the unswerving passage of the seasons. The bustle and din of the market or harbour seem like the heartbeat of some vast, immortal creature, and the organ music accentuates this primary pulse. *Amsterdam* pays tribute to the Jewish quarter of the city, with its three-hundred year tradition of cantor singing. Van der Horst regards the untidiness, the cleanliness, the gaiety, and the stillness, with the tolerance of a poet's gaze. Forever the perfectionist, he reached the summit of his art with this lyrical, pastel-hued documentary.

C. JOHN FERNO

Next to van der Linden and Haanstra in seniority among the great Dutch documentarists of the postwar period, John Ferno (Fernhout in Dutch) began his career earlier than either of them, as assistant to Ivens on *Breakers.* He was only fourteen, and the younger son of a famous Dutch painter, Charley Toorop. Ivens recalls that, "Although he wasn't interested in reading or in abstract knowledge of any kind, he had a very practical sense and a wonderful instinct for the nature and behaviour of everyone with whom he came into contact."[4] Ferno continued to accompany Ivens on his travels, and risked death repeatedly in the streets and fields of Spain during the Civil War, in order to bring to the world the numbing images of *Spanish Earth.* But in 1934, at the age of twenty, he sailed to the South Seas and made *Easter Island,* an astonishingly mature study of the people there, and the legendary statues. The film reminds one strongly of Buñuel's *Las Hurdes* shot two years earlier. Henri Storck edited the piece, and Maurice Jaubert composed the music.

Ferno worked at the National Film Board of Canada, and in the United States, from 1938 onwards and made, among other films, *And So They Live.* Two model documentaries of their kind were his *Broken Dikes (Gebroken dijken,* 1945) and *The Last Shot (Het Laatste schot,* 1945), showing with tragic thoroughness how the artificial island of Walcheren was bombed by the Allies and as a result flooded, so as to flush out the Nazis and gain access to the port of Antwerp, and tracing the difficult period of rehabilitation after the war. Both have an air of bitterness and actuality that is impressive even after thirty years.

In these early films, Ferno reflects the tradition of tough, uncom-

Still from an early film by John Ferno, BLUE PETER

promising cinema that his friend Ivens veered toward in the later
Thirties. Recently, he has resided outside Holland, and his output has
slackened. During the Sixties he produced two 70mm shorts, one
entitled *Fortress of Peace* (1965), which stresses the eternal vigilance of
the Swiss Army in peacetime, and is rich in imaginative flourishes and
mock battles among the mountains, and the other an award-winner at
Cannes, *Sky over Holland* (1967). Here Ferno deploys the panoramic
views from jet aircraft to point a vivid parallel between the Dutch
scenery and the paintings that national artists have produced, from
Cuyp to Mondriaan. The sheer panache of the film disarms the critic:
sound marshalled inventively via six channels; vertiginous, swooping
camera-work (with his son, Douwes Ferno, poised in the nose of a
fighter plane) that ends with an impudent twirl in the clouds; light
and colours changing, blending, giving new significance to a landscape.

The Tree of Life, filmed in Israel in 1971, bears the hallmark of
Ferno's craftsmanship. It is a portrait of a courageous country, but it
also ranges out into the Diaspora, along the branches, so to speak, of
the Jewish community. One feels that Ferno would have dearly liked
to make a feature film, and that here is another talent restricted by the
lack of dramatic ideas and writing in the Netherlands. "Players are too
hard to get," he told me, "because they are all attached to theatre
companies, which are active all over the Netherlands, much more so
than in other countries." Ferno's film-making is a professional skill
second to none; it is sad to see it limited to documentaries like *Delta*

SKY OVER HOLLAND, which won the Grand Prix at Cannes for John Ferno

Data (1968), and to scores of TV films, with their inevitable, built-in obsolescence. When *Sky over Holland* was screened in Cannes, Dutch critics assailed Ferno for promulgating the traditional "tulips and windmills" image of the Netherlands. But that is like blaming a watchmaker for simply not going digital.

John Ferno will probably be remembered first and foremost as an inspired technician. There are worse fates for an artist.

D. HATTUM HOVING

Born in the same year as Ferno, and yet cut down by a mortal sickness while still in his mid-fifties, Hattum Hoving was also a consummate craftsman. But, like the leisurely town of Delft in which he grew up, Hoving was content of character. Content to stay at home, as it were, rather than stalk the world like Ivens or Ferno. For the last twenty years of his life he experimented with sound and vision at the complex of laboratories in Hilversum, known as Cinecentrum, producing a number of intricate documentaries on scientific subjects.

Os Mundi (1960) is an historical survey of electromagnetic energy, witty and instructional by turns. The earlier *Vibro* deals with the casting of concrete piles. *Light* (1971) is a meditation on the natural order of things that ranks with Haanstra's *Panta rhei*. Taking his cue from Haydn's *Creation* music, Hoving celebrates Man's absorption in, and by, light. In a montage of spangled colour visuals, he catches the elusive and all-pervasive function of light in life—light natural, light artificial, light reflective. *The Ocean of Air* (1970) is a refreshing study of the elaborate network controlled by KLM, the Dutch airline, that starts with the historic Dutch urge to carry and travel, and concludes with a notion of Expo 1995 in space. Hoving's discreet dexterity marries together material shot all over the world. *Mixummerdaydream* (1968) is, Hoving told me, "a new attempt to synthesise movement, colour, sound, and image," by reducing the film to the three basic colours and the subsequent shifting of the results. One sees dancers cavorting in different colours against a panchromatic background, and the film becomes truly stimulating when images of the sea or the forest define colours that one never realised formed part of their essence. A flock of birds against the sky is like a handful of confetti tossed through the air.

Sailing (*Zeilen*, 1962) was Hoving's greatest achievement, for it brought his brilliant technique to a far wider audience than he could ever have expected. The sense of freedom, the exultation of the yachtsman as he combats the winds and the waves, are communicated with an unfailing lyricism that recalls John Masefield's sea poems. This entrancing impression of a day's sport took two years to shoot and edit at Cinecentrum and at dozens of locations throughout the Netherlands. *Sailing* (without narration, but enlivened by some spare, electronic music) is imbued with an uncanny rhythm that suggests the assiduous care that Hoving, himself a yachtsman, devoted to his

Hattum Hoving (with beard) directing LIGHT

Still from Hattum Hoving's most popular film, SAILING

subject. It was sold to thirty countries within a year of its release, probably not least on account of the fine colour, imaginatively used but also perfectly processed.

E. FRANS DUPONT AND JAN HULSKER

Another gifted director at work under the aegis of Cinecentrum was Frans Dupont. He began as a pupil of Ivens's, and was engaged on independent productions already in 1934. But by the mid-Sixties he had proved himself the most competent "art film" director in Holland, with *Promise of Heaven (Uitzicht op de hemel,* 1961) and *Portrait of Frans Hals (Portret van Frans Hals,* 1963). The former short is dedicated essentially to stained glass, but is also an analysis of daylight and the subtly differing shades of colour that it can arouse in objects. The striking central sequence shows how, in everyday life, human beings have resorted to the same colours as those of the rainbow— traffic lights, neon signs, and the like demonstrating the point. Dupont uses colour just as exquisitely in his homage to Frans Hals. The film offers a glimpse of a majority of the paintings and concentrates particularly on the severe splendour of the later period; Dupont avoids the trite view of Hals as a joyous, rather careless painter.

An even more penetrating and influential art film was made in 1955 by Dr. Jan Hulsker, later Director-General of Cultural Affairs at

Above: Jan Hulsker (second from left) filming VINCENT VAN GOGH

Above: still from Frans Dupont's PROMISE OF HEAVEN

the Ministry of Arts. *Vincent van Gogh* (1952) was not the first documentary on the Dutch painter (Resnais's Academy Award-winner of 1948 remains the best study of the canvases themselves), but it probes the background to his life with a rare intelligence. Hulsker traces the ferocious tragedy of that career, from the bleak coal mines of Borinage to the burning sunshine of Arles in southern France. How insipid the real landscapes appear beside the angry paintings van Gogh wrought from them! The commentary is taken from the artist's letters to his elder brother, Theo, who sustained him financially in all seasons; and Hulsker notes with irony the posthumous fame and fortune that so eluded van Gogh in his lifetime. The same director, incidentally, paid tribute to another great countryman in *Erasmus: the Voice of Reason* (*Erasmus, de stem van de rede,* 1961).

F. THEO VAN HAREN NOMAN

The Polygoon-Profilti Newsreel succoured many a talented Dutch film-maker in the years after the war. Theo van Haren Noman was one of the first cameramen to work there in 1946, and five years later he became a freelance director and producer. Two of his films are outstanding, one as an almost flawless example of the Dutch documentary, the other as an experiment with memory and subjective camerawork.

An Army of Hewn Stone (Een leger van gehouwen steen, 1957) amounts

Still from Theo van Haren Noman's AN ARMY OF HEWN STONE

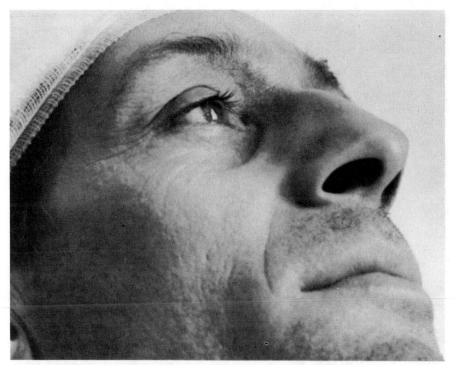

Still from THE INJURED MAN

to a poignant lament for Dutchmen killed in the Second World War. The text is composed of fragments from Resistance poems, and these stirring lines are read in visual rhyme with shots of stone sculpture, statues whose sightless eyes implore the spectator to heed their pain, their desecration, at the hands of the Nazis. Van Haren Noman's choice of camera angle is unnervingly effective; the statues seem to live, to loom over one like soldiers frozen against the busy sky. This is a film that harnesses a tradition of craftsmanship to a keenly-felt indignation at the viciousness and hypocrisy of war.

In *The Injured Man* (*De gewonde*, 1966), fragments of fantasy and reality coalesce as a man begins his journey down towards death after an accident. The images are uncertain and ephemeral, expressing the patient's inability to communicate. The soundtrack, with its dislocating bursts of music, reinforces the sense of claustrophobia. The hospital is composed of menacing shadows and the delirious patient is wheeled down corridors that threaten to cave in upon him. This film is disturbing in a particularly surrealist fashion. There is no longer any barrier between dream and actuality.

G. JAN VRIJMAN

The more talented he is, the more a Dutch director tests the resilience of the traditional documentary mode. From the beginning of his career, Jan Vrijman has been something of an *enfant terrible;* each of

Impasto work taken to its extremes, in THE REALITY OF KAREL APPEL

his films has exhibited flashes of originality and non-conformism. *The Reality of Karel Appel (De werkelijkheid van Karel Appel, 1962)* won the Golden Bear for shorts at the Berlinale, and established Vrijman's name on the Dutch scene. If ever a film allowed the modern action painter to expose his petty self, this one does. Appel's method is to slap great lumps of paint on a gigantic canvas, squeezing his tubes of colour with pretentious venom. One exterior sequence shows the depressing environment that stimulates Appel to declare himself in this manner. "I paint like a barbarian in a barbaric age," he claims, and Vrijman's camera watches him attack his subject. There is a suitably anarchic score by Dizzy Gillespie, based on Appel's own rantings.

Ranting of a different order was featured in Vrijman's candid camera study of revivalism, buskers and others such, *On the Bottom Rung of Heaven* (*Op de bodem van de hemel*, 1965), a kind of forerunner to *Marjoe*, and his provocative investigation of the agency ethos, *Identity—Confessions of an Ad Addict* (1971), was another step forward. Vrijman, however, spent the late Sixties and early Seventies building up an independent Dutch feature film company—Cineproductie. He financed, or helped to finance, such films as Weisz's *Illusion is a Gangster Girl* and Hugo Claus's *The Enemies* (see Chapter Seven). "I am resolved," he told me in 1972, "to design a feature film formula that is not vulgar but is nonetheless commercially acceptable." He never did. But Cineproductie was responsible for interesting shorts on subjects like science, art, education, and psychology. Vrijman has always felt an overwhelming need to project strong ideas and philosophies, and to focus in particular on the significance of minority groups in modern society.

Still from THE MAKING OF A BALLET, directed by Jan Vrijman

In 1969, he conceived one of the most successful film ventures ever
to emerge from the Netherlands—"Holland 70," the multi-screen
presentation that dominated the Dutch pavilion at EXPO in Osaka. A
British expert on multimedia and president of Europe's largest
design organisation, James Pilditch, described it as "a masterpiece of
visual art . . . you rise on a series of escalators through walls of film
and sound." The magazine *Japan Architect* commented, "Though the
screens are numerous, a simplification system reduces their content
to an orderly set of stories and thereby increases their effectiveness.
This straight-forward, restrained approach to multi-projection is
much more than the flood of images and sounds used in many other
pavilions." Vrijman worked like a demon on the Osaka project,
blending the talents of Frans Weisz, the director, Anton van Munster,
the cinematographer, Massimo Götz, the art director, and Paul Roof,
the editor. One cannot think of another Dutch team with sufficient
verve and optimism to have carried it off so well.

In 1973, Vrijman returned to directing, and *The Making of a Ballet*,
which describes the work and personality of Rudi van Dantzig, is his
most satisfying work since *Karel Appel*—to which it bears a conspicuous resemblance in its quest for the motive force that animates an
artist like van Dantzig. Vrijman intercuts rehearsals for the choreog-
rapher's ballet, "Painted Birds," with shots of the finished performance. The restless cutting and the flawless lighting counterpoint the
violence, power, and disenchantment of van Dantzig's vision.

H. NICO CRAMA

A more diffident personality than Vrijman, but a personality
nonetheless indispensable to the Dutch cinema, is Nico Crama. As
well as directing several impeccably-tooled documentaries himself, he
has produced shorts such as Jan Oonk's *The Marble*, Paul Verhoeven's
The Wrestler, and Zwartjes's *It's Me*, which have been screened in
numerous countries. He has also played a leading role in organising
"Holland Animation" (see Chapter Nine). At the age of sixteen, he
went to Paris and made an 8mm documentary on the city, travelling
through the streets by bicycle. His work was noted, and he was offered
a scholarship to the French film school, IDHEC.

In an already prolific career, Crama's two outstanding ac-
complishments are *Piet Mondriaan* and *Daumier, Eye Witness of an
Epoch*. With an intelligent commentary and soundtrack by Mart
Ambry, the Daumier film evokes the influence of the great
Nineteenth-century artist.

For his Mondriaan documentary, Crama worked in collaboration
with the Municipal Museum in The Hague, which houses the most
important collection of the painter's canvases. The film follows
Mondriaan's evolution through naturalism and cubism towards a
pure form of abstraction. Even the artist's studio resembles one of his

*Above: Nico Crama directing his documentary, PIET MONDRIAAN (photo
Frederick Linck Studio)*

Above: still from DAUMIER, EYE WITNESS OF AN EPOCH

ascetic, rectilinear paintings. Crama's combination of sounds, commentary, and analysis unlocks Mondriaan's seemingly inhuman world. The paintings become more eloquent, the artist more sympathetic, than ever before. An earlier Crama documentary, also made in asssociation with the Municipal Museum in The Hague, traces the growth of the photographic portrait, from Sarah Bernhardt to Winston Churchill. *Photo Portrait* (1970) deploys the most modern visual technique available, to illustrate this progress in photography since 1840.

Crama's talents have been recognised by the National Film Board of Canada, where he has worked on assignment twice in recent years. One of the most widely-booked of his shorts is *Douwe van den Berg, Undesirable* (*Douwe van den Berg, ongewenst,* 1972), which deals with the rehabilitation of prisoners. He is now completing a film for the National Film Board on the nearly half million Dutch-Canadians who live in North America. "Dutch facilities are all very fine," he says, "but the abiding problem in Holland is one of money. The government tries to be generous, but films are *so* expensive, and as an independent producer I have always had to fight for more finance."

I. OTHER TALENTS

Two other art documentaries deserve mention in any survey of recent Dutch film. *Adventures in Perception* (*Het oog op avontuur,* 1970), by

Painting used in Jonne Severijn's a PAUSE IN TIME

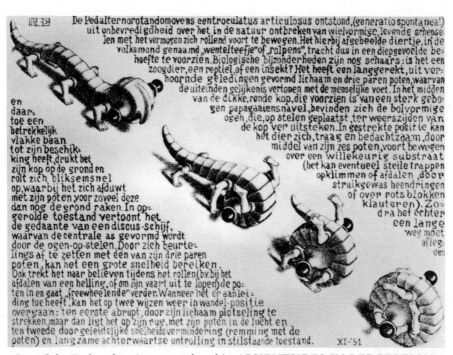

De Pedalternorotandomovens centroculatus articulosus ontstond,(generatio spontanea!) uit onbevredigdheid over het in de natuur ontbreken van wielvormige, levende schepse len met het vermogen zich rollend voort te bewegen.Het hierbij afgebeelde diertje,in de volksmond genaamd „wentelteefje"of „rolpens", tracht dus in een diepgevoelde be= hoefte te voorzien.Biologische bijzonderheden zijn nog schaars :is het een zoogdier,een reptiel,of een insekt?Het heeft een langgerekt,uit ver= hoornde geledingen gevormd lichaam en drie paren poten,waarvan de uiteinden gelijkenis vertonen met de menselijke voet.In het midden van de dikke,ronde kop,die voorzien is van een sterk gebo= gen papagaaiensnavel,bevinden zich de bolvormige ogen,die,op stelen geplaatst ,ter weerszijden van de kop ver uitsteken.In gestrekte positie kan het dier zich,traag en bedachtzaam ,door middel van zijn zes poten,voort bewegen over een willekeurig substraat (het kan eventueel steile trappen opklimmen of afdalen ,door struikgewas heendringen of over rotsblokken klauteren).Zo= dra het echter een lange weg moet afleg= gen

en daar= toe een betrekkelijk vlakke baan tot zijn beschik= king heeft,drukt het zijn kop op de grond en rolt zich bliksemsnel op,waarbij het zich afduwt met zijn poten voor zoveel deze dan nog de grond raken.In op= gerolde toestand vertoont het de gedaante van een discus-schijf, waarvan de centrale as gevormd wordt door de ogen-op-stelen.Door zich beurte= lings af te zetten met één van zijn drie paren poten,kan het een grote snelheid bereiken. Ook trekt het naar believen tijdens het rollen(bv.bij het afdalen van een helling,of om zijn vaart uit te lopen)de po= ten in en gaat „freewheelende"verder.Wanneer het er aanlei= ding toe heeft,kan het op twee wijzen weer in wandel-positie overgaan: ten eerste abrupt,door zijn lichaam plotseling te strekken,maar dan ligt het op zijn rug,met zijn poten in de lucht en ten tweede door geleidelijke snelheidsvermindering (remming met de poten) en langzame achterwaartse ontrolling in stilstaande toestand.   XI-'51

One of the Escher drawings reproduced in ADVENTURES IN PERCEPTION

Han van Gelder, deals with the tantalising designs of Maurits Escher. Gelder blocks off slabs of the screen from time to time in order to give a clue to Escher's illusory perspectives. Mirror images are achieved in a single, flat dimension. Stairways continue to infinity; floors become ceilings. Van Gelder's brilliant treatment of these drawings simultaneously enhances their mystery and reveals their calculation.

Jonne Severijn, long respected as a specialist in this field, pays tribute to the life and output of an unjustly neglected Italian artist Giovanni Boldini, in *A Pause in Time (Een gat in de tijd,* 1974). He does so through a series of dialogues with Boldini's widow, who was a young journalist when she fell in love with, and married, the painter (himself nearly ninety at the time). The documentary transcends its rather mundane format by virtue of the affection and warmth so clearly felt by Severijn for this forgotten maestro. He conjures up the atmosphere of Paris in the Belle Epoque, where Boldini made friends with Degas, and the dead man's spirit seems somehow to endure in the tranquil sunlight of the villa where his widow still lives.

Many of the better Dutch documentarists have undergone their apprenticeship outside Holland. Fons Grasveld spent several months on a scholarship visit to Poland, and worked with Zanussi on *Illumination,* as well as directing *A Day in the Life of a Warsaw Busdriver* (*Warszawski kierowca Jerzy Winnicki,* 1973), which was well-received at the Oberhausen Festival. His experimental works in the Netherlands

Still from OH, I SEE . . . , directed by Fons Grasveld

are concerned with the welfare of ordinary people in a world where their opinions are frequently ignored or dismissed. *Blood* (*Bloed,* 1973) is a dramatised documentary on the dangers of nuclear power, *Oh, I See . . .* (*O, moet dat zo,* 1975) sympathises with the mentally handicapped, *Roadsweeper* (*Gijs van Groenestein, Straatveger,* 1976) is a profile of a manual worker in the big city, and *Do I Really Want to Die?* (*Wil ik wel dood?,* 1974) is a frank and sensible confrontation with the problem of suicide.

Other documentaries are notable on account of their solitary achievement rather than as phases in a director's career. One thinks, for example, of Jan van der Hoeven's *Sunday Sun* (*Zon op Zondag,* 1964), a quiet, Olmi-like impression of Sunday morning in a Dutch town. In the ghostly dawn the early risers fish beside a stream; a young couple cavort about the deserted streets; a man and his family set out for a picnic in a battered car. The observation is sharp and humane, and the jazz score helps the rhythm of this likeable little film.

Or of *Aqua di Roma* (1973), by Boud Smit, another mood piece, with water as its theme—rain water, water in the Roman fountains, water in the pipes that serve a huge city. The photography (by Anton van Munster and Jan Oonk) conveys with an almost physical impact the heat of the Italian streets and the sense of relief when a thunderstorm quenches all needs, from washing clothes to scrubbing statues.

Or of *Den Haag Holland* (1968), directed by Caspar Willers from a script by Gerard J. Raucamp (who himself has been one of the most efficient and versatile of the Dutch documentarists during the past fifteen years). This attractive short provides a multi-faceted picture of the Dutch capital, leavening the usual tourist film approach with touches of sly humour that are the trademark of Raucamp's productions.

Statue from Gerard Raucamp's production of DEN HAAG, HOLLAND, directed by Caspar Willers

Max Croiset and Jan Teulings in VILLAGE ON THE RIVER

6. THE WORLD OF FONS RADEMAKERS

> "Any Dutch film director not con-
> tent to make a lyrical film is forced to
> thrust his own fragment of drama
> on an essentially recalcitrant
> background"
> —Jan Blokker

Only one man in Holland since the war has managed to build a career in feature films spanning more than twenty years, and for many foreign audiences the work of Fons Rademakers remains the only glimpse they have caught of Dutch cinema. Not for Rademakers the traditional documentary approach to life; his is a world of dreams and aspirations, nightmare and fantasy, not far removed from that of Ingmar Bergman, who he knows and whose films he loved at a significant stage in his own career.

Rademakers is an eminently civilised man, imbued with the culture of his native Low Countries, but also widely versed in world literature and art, equally at home in France or the United States, Indonesia or Sweden. His father was a doctor and later a philosopher. The entire family was by lineage devoted to medicine, but Fons fell in love with the movies (and, coincidentally, with the daughter of a local cinema owner in Roosendaal), and felt that the best way of entering the film field was to become an actor. His parents were Francophiles and urged him to study acting in Paris.

The war intervened. Rademakers served in the army, and then returned to acting. He was arrested for harbouring Jews, but released by a mayor who had known him and liked his work as an actor. Fons travelled to Switzerland, met Jacques Feyder, and played Raskolnikov to Michel Simon's Porphyrius in the Frenchman's stage production of *Crime and Punishment*. Through Simon, he was introduced to Jean-Louis Barrault and determined to settle in Paris, at that period the heart of the theatrical world. He returned to Holland at Christmas, 1944, and told his parents of his decision.

This commitment to a stage career was paramount in Rademakers until his mid-thirties. From acting he had progressed to some impressive productions of his own (Büchner's *Danton's Death,* a farce by Feydeau, and Victrac's *Victor).* Then, as he has always done, Rademakers began travelling again. He learned the practical details of film-making with Fellini and De Sica (he was assistant on *Il tetto*) in Italy,

with David Lean in England, and with Jacques Becker in Paris. When
he came back to the Netherlands, he began writing his first feature,
Village on the River (Dorp aan de rivier (1958) with the Belgian novelist,
Hugo Claus, from the well-known book by Anton Coolen. Rademakers, like Harry Kümel, has sought to draw on the best resources
and qualities of both Holland and Belgium, bringing together cultures that were once united. Through his admiration for Bergman,
however, he injected into the somewhat stolid material of this first film
a Scandinavian sense of the dark forces that lie beyond the fringe of
everyday experience, and a corresponding visual style, born of
chiaroscuro lighting and crepuscular exteriors.

"Film," says Rademakers, "is, as far as I am concerned, telling a
story." *Village on the River* describes a captious doctor who wilfully sets
up a barrier of cynicism and disdain between himself and his patients.
He reads a newspaper while a man's wife is in the last throes of
childbirth, and in the nick of time delivers the baby. In the eyes of the
community he is "a peculiar gent," stubborn, humourless, resolute—
ready if necessary to plunge across the icy Meuse by night to save a
patient. When his own wife ails, he softens a little, listening to her
anxious, naïve expressions of fear and insecurity. She dies, and the
doctor shows his children the corpse in the open coffin. In the film's
most gripping sequence, the young son watches through an upstairs
window as the doctor and a friend bury the woman's body by night in
the garden (Rademakers uses a slow zoom with real intelligence and
dramatic timing here, a device rare in 1958).

The pleasures of *Village on the River* stem from the characters—deaf
Cis, who narrates the film, and the gypsy woman who comes ravenous
to his barge; local menfolk gossiping around the bier of a suicide.
Death inspires a particular awe in this Catholic region of the Netherlands.

The film was nominated for an Academy Award in Hollywood, and
earned Rademakers a name among arthouse devotees outside Holland. *That Joyous Eve . . . (Makers staakt uw wild geraas,* 1960) was a
comedy with serious overtones, revolving round three families at the
time of the St. Nicholas festival, which in the Low Countries means all
the uproarious celebrations associated with Christmas in Britain or
Thanksgiving in the United States. Rademakers was again able to
draw on his boyhood memories of Dutch winter evenings, but with
irony rather than sentimentality. One might say that Rademakers's
cosmopolitan personality permits him to view with detachment a type
of existence that he loves and cherishes.

The Knife (Het mes, 1961), the first of the films to be shot by
Rademakers in scope ratio, is a convincing view of life through the
eyes of a boy, and contains a dream scene that reminds one of similar
Freudian excursions in Bergman's early period. Based on a short
story, *The Knife* shows how a child in the midst of puberty reacts to his

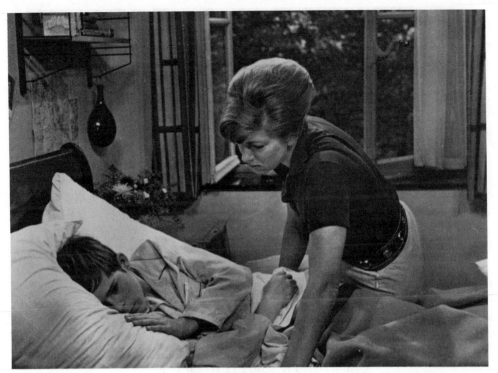

Still from THE KNIFE

parents' own transgressions (the wife has a lover) and regards the heavily symbolic knife as a dangerous and thrilling prize. The young actor playing Thomas is a trifle wooden, but the jazz score reinforces the mood of emotional confusion that governs the film.

The Spitting Image (*Als twee druppels water,* 1963) was a considerable success in Holland; less so abroad (though John Le Carré is among its admirers). Its fundamental dilemma—a man's search for his identity—gives the clue to Rademakers's *Weltanschauung* (which coincided well with that of W. F. Hermans, on whose novel, "The Dark Room of Damocles," the film was based). His most ambitious work has always sprung from the premise that a man must come to terms with his personality if he is to achieve fulfilment and peace of mind. Ducker in *The Spitting Image* finds himself shadowed by a "double," whose misdeeds bring his own character into question. Like Losey's Mr. Klein, he is demoralised and obsessed by the situation, trying desperately to track down his *alter ego* among the anonymous streets and rail stations of urban Holland. In wartime, when the Dutch Resistance required no knowledge of one's background, only a capacity for "doing the job," Ducker can cope with his profound inferiority complex. When the fighting is over, though, such anonymity is shed, and Ducker is arrested in England as a spy. Eventually he is shot down as he runs demented through the grounds of a detention centre.

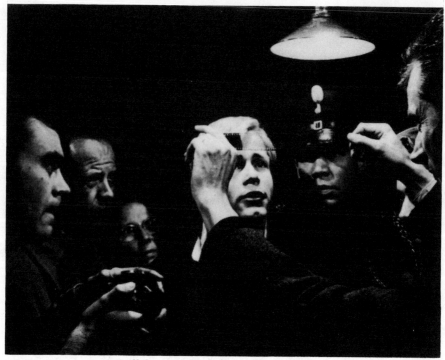

Still from THE SPITTING IMAGE

Rademakers directs the film with admirable smoothness, and builds the suspense steadily to a climax. At the beginning, the tone of the acting is excitable, the lines melodramatic, but little by little the enigmatic atmosphere grows more persuasive; the distinction between truth and propaganda, between the halves of Ducker's identity, blur and overlap like those of Alma and Elisabet in *Persona* or Dr. Jekyll and Mr. Hyde. There is something satanic about the end of the film, when the boy's girlfriend is seen on a beach with the *sosie*, unaware of his genuine identity. As Rademakers says, the uncanny implication of *The Spitting Image* is that if, in war, you are on one side you are a hero, on the other a villain.

Oscar Rosander, the great Swedish editor, had helped Rademakers cut *Village on the River.* Now, in the mid-Sixties, Rademakers turned to another Bergman colleague, Gunnel Lindblom, for the leading role in *The Dance of the Heron* (*De dans van de reiger,* 1966). The international flavour of the film was heightened by the presence of Sacha Vierny as cinematographer, and Jean Desailly as Edouard, with the entire production being shot on location near Dubrovnik. All this is appropriate, for the central characters in *Dance of the Heron* are literally, as well as psychologically, deracinated. The husband, Edouard, is suspicious and chary of his beautiful wife, and she in turn is intoxicated by the *alfresco* brilliance of the Adriatic coast, the ceaseless sunshine, the nights of carousing and dancing in the streets

and piazzas. She allows herself to be courted by a local sailor,
deliberately provoking Edouard into some kind of reaction until, with
his stern, supercilious features and formal attire he assumes comic
dimensions. Edouard is the classic cuckold, around whom the
"heron" weaves her dance in a mood of bitterness and enticement.
Immobility is death, wrote Multatuli. Rademakers agrees; and until
Edouard reacts to his wife's provocation, he is doomed. The obvious
portentousness of the plot is undercut by sequences that catch the
absurdist quality of Hugo Claus's original play. Edouard imagines
himself suffering a heart attack at the end of a holiday, and how on
the way home his body is stolen on a Yugoslav road; later he decides to
hang himself, aided and abetted by his mother.

If *Dance of the Heron* fails to impress as much as it should, it is
probably due on the one hand to the unplausible nature of the
marriage, and one the other to the intensity that Rademakers so
clearly feels and yet cannot quite communicate. Jan Troell fell short
in a similar fashion with *Bang!* Nothing, it seems, is more difficult to
analyse than the male menopause.

After a space of five years, Rademakers returned to the screen with
a box-office triumph, drawn from a book by the well-loved Flemish
author, Stijn Streuvels. *Mira* (1971) was co-produced with Belgium,
and filmed there. It introduced the nubile figure of Willeke van

Gunnel Lindblom in DANCE OF THE HERON

Ammelrooy, and revealed a sensuality and bucolic wit in Rade-makers's direction. There are plans for a bridge to be built across a river, and the villagers on one bank are incensed. The deacon threatens to stave in the head of the first man who helps the construction team. Lander, a local youth, comes home from army service and is im-mediately struck by Mira; there is a genuine erotic charge to the scene where he brings her out of the river and she lies on the bank, her body exposed beneath white scraps of blouse and skirt. But Lander drowns two of the government surveyors, and is soon rounded up by mounted police in a sequence that prefigures *Max Havelaar* and underlines Fons's admiration for Kurosawa—the fleeing man, his pursuers, and the sylvan landscape blending in a blur of fluent tracking shots.

Mira contains elements of the quixotic and the tragic. Rademakers likes to keep the audience on its toes, wondering which way the mood, rather than the story, will go next. He himself plays a pompous functionary who tries to justify the building scheme, only to be debagged by the furious crowd in a local tavern. Of course progress is inexorable, and it is left to Mira herself to do the two things that the community regards as least likely: marry, and cut the ribbon inau-gurating the new bridge . . . Willeke van Ammelrooy portrays Mira as an earth spirit, who slips like quicksilver through the fingers of everyone who yearns for her, and Georges Delerue contributes a score that is by turns tender and rollicking, matching the aims of a film that offers a Gallic charm habitually lacking in Dutch cinema.

Because of the Cats, a contemporary thriller directed by Rademakers in 1973, is best forgotten. Marred by poor acting and a series of overheated situations, the film did little for its director's reputation other than to confirm his professional craftsmanship. Three years later, however, Rademakers was to achieve the greatest success of his life . . .

*   *   *

Eduard Douwes Dekker (under the pseudonym of Multatuli) wrote *Max Havelaar* in 1859, in the wake of a disastrous experience in Java, where he had been appalled by the degree of corruption among the native population and the Dutch colonial rulers. *Havelaar* is patently autobiographical; but its deceptively inchoate structure, composed of dramatic moments interspersed with comments on the state of the coffee market in Amsterdam, and with prolix asides on the condition of the Indonesian roads, enabled Multatuli to convey the unmitigated truth of the matter: that the Netherlands had acquiesced in a foul situation and that anyone who sought to eliminate these abuses was stifled by the power and indifference of the establishment. D.H. Lawrence and Henry Miller are just two of the foreign authors who regard *Max Havelaar* as a classic. Read today, it evinces a suppleness of thought and sophistication of style that make most other Nineteenth-century novels appear crude by comparison.

Rademakers had long dreamed of filming this subtle book. He knew Indonesia well, and was at last able to sign a co-production contract with P.T. Mondial Motion Pictures in Jakarta. Authentic locations were vital to the success of the venture. Rademakers even found the actual house in central Java where Havelaar/Multatuli was stationed; nowadays it is owned by the very prince who in the film plays a devious Regent. The Governor-General's mansion, an image of grace and authority deployed by Rademakers with irony at crucial points in the film, was occupied—and much loved—by the late President Soekarno.

Rademakers steeped himself in the life of Indonesia. He prepared and rehearsed the film for six months prior to a hectic sixteen-week shooting schedule, with a further ten days of studio work in Holland. He had written the script in partnership with Gerard Soeteman, who in the past few years has emerged as one of the few competent, professional Dutch screenwriters.

The result of this immense physical and mental effort is not only the crowning achievement of Fons's career, but also the most imposing fiction film ever produced in the Netherlands.

Why?

There is nothing unusual about an anti-colonialist movie in these disillusioned times. It is easy to condemn imperialism and leave the matter at that. The greatness of Multatuli's (and Rademakers's) vision is that he assigns the guilt to no individual or country; corruption and prejudice are embedded deep in human nature and are manifest at every level of society. Havelaar may rail and struggle against the *status quo,* but eventually he must resign from the service if he is to preserve his integrity.

Rademakers astutely rhymes the dramatic tension of the story with the mounting moral exasperation that afflicts Havelaar. The novel starts leisurely, almost sluggishly; but the film breaks immediately into a gallop with two incidents—the theft of a much-loved buffalo from a native boy, Saidjah, and the poisoning of Havelaar's predecessor, Slotering, at a banquet given by the local Regent. One is aware of the unadorned virulence of the jungle. A tiger springs upon a buffalo and there is a terrible fight. When Slotering dies, there is no escaping the horror of his final pangs; he twists slowly into a foetal crouch, as though reduced once more to the womb. From this point onwards, the environment exudes a menacing character even by day. Nature is a physical presence in the film; one has a sense of pitfalls on every side; one feels, with Havelaar, the hostility not only of the people but of the forest too. By night, the house with its Dutch family is like a fragile ark. The light wards off danger, but beyond the range of the lamps lie dark, ferocious thoughts and threats. When Havelaar's little

Peter Faber in MAX HAVELAAR

son is intimidated by snakes in the garden, one suspects that the external world itself has turned against the intruders. And in the sub-plot involving Saidjah, Rademakers sets up a deadly pursuit through the forest, as the Regent's riders hunt down the two serfs. During this breathless chase, one is never quite certain which is the more savage antagonist—man or the landscape in which he moves.

Peter Faber creates a three-dimensional Havelaar. He stands out from his fellow functionaries by virtue of his proud, assertive gaze, and his dynamic conduct. In his opening address to the assembled chiefs and colleagues at the station, he breaks one colonialist taboo after another. "If we paid the chiefs well, they would not have to steal from the people." Nature, hunger, thoughts, ideas exist more vividly for Havelaar than do buildings or museums. Married to a plain, loyal wife, he dreams of pretty girls in France but clings to his family responsibilities. Havelaar's refusal to compromise, allied to his impetuous character (illustrated wittily in various episodes), drag him into mortal combat with the "system." The Controller in Labak is craven and impotent; the Resident kowtows to the Regent and purchases his good offices; even the Governor is afraid to confront Havelaar when he arrives at the mansion. Connivance and prevarication are all. Trapped in an ante-room, Havelaar finds himself almost blinded by bright sunlight streaming in through the windows. He is a moral, if not yet a physical prisoner. Turning, he seizes a portrait of the Dutch King, William III, and inveighs against him for the state of affairs in Java. Rademakers dissolves from the painting to the face of Drystibble and others at worship in the Grote Kerk in Amsterdam. The camera tracks in accusation along row after row of pious burghers. On the soundtrack the hymn-singing grows louder and louder, prevailing over Havelaar and his frustration like a huge, annihilating force.

It is a stunning conclusion. Never in the cinema has the insidious alliance between religious zeal and colonial exploitation—the one masking and justifying the other—been presented with such deadly skill. As the story proceeds, one wonders when Rademakers will make a false step. But he avoids the familiar hazards of the epic genre. He does not stress the folkloric aspects. He eschews sentimentality when dealing with Saidjah and his death at the hands of mercenaries. He sketches with bold strokes the outlines of a compassionate marriage, not a glamorous romance, between Havelaar and his wife. Above all, he uses his exotic setting as an essential ingredient of his theme rather than as a mere backdrop. Rademakers, like Multatuli, condemns not so much the Dutch or the Javanese chiefs as the superiority complex that lurks, ready to be awakened, in the minds of all men at all times.

Multatuli would have been stirred by this angry, engrossing film.

7. THE LONG NEW WAVE

A. INTRODUCTION

Between the Liberation of 1945 and the establishment of the Netherlands Film Academy in 1958, the Dutch cinema was represented almost exclusively by the documentary. But Anton Koolhaas, presently head of that Academy, gave a sign of better things to come when he made *The Dike is Sealed* (*De dijk is dicht,* 1959). Like *Six Years,* it recaptures the Dutch wartime atmosphere, but its sense of pace and depth of feeling are more convincing. A young man, Bert, whose wife has perished during the bombing of Walcheren, returns to the island and appreciates that life must continue, and that by devoting himself to the rehabilitation of this little Protestant community, he can also recover his own will to live. Koolhaas deploys darkness and shadows extremely well to suggest the clandestine adventures of Bert and his colleagues. There are some fortuitous dramatic interventions, such as the appearance of a saviour just as Bert is about to commit suicide, but there are also incidents of sickening logic, such as the slow, inexorable inundation of an old mill where several folk are trapped after a bombardment.

The closing scenes of *The Dike is Sealed,* with new lives, new crops

Postwar optimism in the Dutch cinema: THE DIKE IS SEALED

taking root, while the famous Walcheren lighthouse swings its eternal gaze over the seascape, might well symbolise the arrival of a new wave in Dutch film. Hans Saaltink has written that, "The founding of the Netherlands Film Academy in 1958 was an important landmark. It meant that a new generation was also to learn the theory of film-making instead of having to rely solely on practical experience."[5] Television, rapidly gaining ground in the nation, provided the young directors with technicians and actors who were accustomed to the cameras. The magazine "Skoop," launched in 1964, offered ample terrain for debate about the aims and achievements of the new film-makers. The magazine was effervescent and opinionated, de-fending films like *A bout de souffle* and *L'avventura,* which had received short shrift from the established reviewers. Nikolai van der Heyde, Frans Weisz, Adriaan Ditvoorst, Pim de la Parra, Wim Verstappen and their friends were united in their determination to reject the documentary image of Holland as a country of dikes, cheese, and tulips. Most creative writers regard the short story as an exercise for—or relaxation from—their novels. Painters are rarely satisfied with mere drawings or lithographs, even though they need to do them for a living. So the film-maker thinks of his shorts, and it is scarcely surprising that during the Sixties in Holland there was a rebellion against the long-established tradition of shorts and shorts alone.

In many respects, however, that revolt has become a Pyrrhic victory. Dutch audiences had always assumed that films, like cars and watches, were best imported from abroad. They were, quite literally, unaccustomed to hearing their own language spoken on the screen. Hardly any Dutch feature fared well financially during the Sixties, and some collapsed at the box-office like pricked balloons, prompting Remco Campert, the writer, to declare at the close of the decade that, "The Dutch feature film situation is like a monk's self-immolation. It is noble, it is terrible to behold, and it leaves nothing behind." Even *Monsieur Hawarden* (1968), a brilliant reconstruction of Nineteenth-century life in the Low Countries, and an invited entry to the London Film Festival, had to be withdrawn from Amsterdam's big cinema, the Calypso, after only a brief run. Not unexpectedly, the director, Harry Kümel, returned to his native Belgium, while the producer, Rob du Mée, one of the few dedicated supporters of the new film movement in the Netherlands, struggled on for a few more years like a weary crusader, until he could no longer absorb both the losses and the consistent reminders of failure.

Another independent producer, Jan Vrijman, was among the first to see the potential of shooting Dutch films with English dialogue, but even this could not sway the indifference of the Dutch cinemagoer. *The Enemies* (*De vijanden,* 1968) was another disaster, afflicted with the inevitable hazards of dubbing and various other lapses from technical excellence. Hugo Claus, a novelist, made his *début* as a director and discounted criticism of the movie's simplistic conversations by assert-ing that, "It's an attempt to adapt the technique of the comic strip to the cinema. The characters are deliberately given banal lines of

Ellen Vogel in Harry Kümel's MONSIEUR HAWARDEN

dialogue, like the bubble-talk in comics." Certainly the most impressive aspect of *The Enemies* is its accumulation of unpredictable incidents, as confusing as war really is, and linked by dissolves rather than cuts, so that the effect is one of telescoped time.

In this atmosphere of failure, few directors had either the courage or the resources to nourish a steady career in feature films. Men like Philo Bregstein, with *The Compromise* (*Het compromis*, 1968), which won a prize at the Venice Festival, Erik Terpstra, who directed what he termed "a funny, hip, cruel, modern comedy" in *The Whipping Cream Hero* (*De verloedering van de Swieps*, 1967), and Renée Daalder, with *The White Slave* (*De blanke slavin*, 1969), all had to abandon their ambitious programmes. Daalder at least escaped from Holland to Hollywood, where he was responsible for an exploitation movie, *Massacre at Central High*, unworthy of his talent.

Various ancillary reasons for this disappointing situation were advanced by the pundits. Professional producers of the calibre of Rudy Meyer ("the finest producer Holland ever had," says Charles Huguenot van der Linden) were lacking. There were no indigenous screenwriters. The critics themselves were unduly intolerant of the technical disabilities that marred most of the new features. In time, of course, all these flaws were eradicated, and a steady number of reasonably successful Dutch films are released theatrically every year. The government film budget is increased annually. A Netherlands entry in the competitive section of each major festival is now a regular occurrence, and not the fluke of yesteryear. But the wounds have healed slowly, and the concept of a native cinema still alienates the Dutch. "I detest national cinemas, and national boundaries," maintained Nikolai van der Heyde a few years back.

There is not space in this modest survey to discuss every Dutch feature of the past twelve years. Some films, by directors as diverse as Samuel Meyering, Roeland Kerbosch, and Ate de Jong, I have not seen. Others are omitted because by the searching standards of international cinema they are simply not very good.

B. NIKOLAI VAN DER HEYDE

The blithest figure in the Dutch new wave is Nikolai van der Heyde. An incorrigible romantic, he achieves height of lyricism in his films, which match the mood of Bo Widerberg (whose cinematographer, Jörgen Persson, he has employed on various occasions). Perhaps, if there had been a more positive tradition of cinema in the Netherlands, van der Heyde might have found the necessary self-confidence to pursue the path taken by Widerberg in Sweden. There are sequences in each of his movies that reveal a quite undeniable talent, an ability to express human feelings in sound and imagery that soar above the worthy norm.

Van der Heyde, like Weisz, Verstappen, de la Parra and others, was

Still from Nikolai van der Heyde's A MORNING OF SIX WEEKS

an early graduate of the Netherlands Film Academy and an active writer in "Skoop." While still a student, he wrote and directed *The Bowling Alley,* a short that won a prize at the CINESTUD International Festival in 1963. Three years later, his first feature, *A Morning of Six Weeks (Een ochtend van zes weken)* was released, and struck critics with its sensuality and *élan.* The story concerns the love affair between a Parisian model and a Dutch racing driver. She is visiting Amsterdam with her small son, and cherishes the affection of the solid, serious Dutchman. Both of them try to delay the end of the relationship, and there is a flood of misunderstandings. The film is composed of flashbacks as Jimmy, the racing driver, chats to a new mistress at dawn. The plot is neither spectacular nor unfamiliar. But van der Heyde fills his movie with compassion, and sadness tugs at the affair in even its lightest moments. Locations, especially the airport and the chill house where the lovers quarrel at the end, dictate the mood of a scene with the same intensity as they do in Truffaut's work. The language barrier—the girl speaks only French—is also exploited tactfully, although there are some awkward lines when an English radio interviewer invades the race track. There is a melancholy truthfulness about the whole piece that lingers and grows in the mind long after one's initial admiration for Gerard Vandenberg's photography has subsided.

A Morning of Six Weeks was made on a budget of merely $35,000;

Barbara Seagull Sandy van der Linden in LOVE COMES QUIETLY . . .

clearly van der Heyde had learnt his craft with care and economy. He had spent much time during the early Sixties with directors like Chabrol, Donen, and Autant-Lara. "I despise the Dutch audience, who only love Louis de Funès," he told me in 1968, the year of the student uprising in France and the year that saw the release of van der Heyde's second feature, *To Grab the Ring.* It was a miserable flop at the box-office, and suffered from poor post-synchronisation in English. This blemish apart, *To Grab the Ring* is technically competent, again brilliantly and intimately photographed by Vandenberg. It is the drama of an American in his early thirties. Alfred Lowell (Ben Carruthers) is tempted back to Europe by a petty gangster and tries to retrieve the threads of a relationship he enjoyed five years earlier with a Frenchwoman (Françoise Brion). Lowell has a facility for seducing pretty girls *en passant,* but he is deeply unhappy. "I'm not as wise as I could be," he says after a bout of love-making. "I resent the kids having fun." Thus the film is sustained by his fear of growing old, of slipping out of key with a fresh generation.

In the past ten years, van der Heyde has produced two further films of high calibre; the balance of his output is more kindly to be forgotten, a symptom not so much of his own inadequacies as of the spasmodic progress of modern Dutch cinema. *Love Comes Quietly . . .* (1973, also known as *Angela*) re-established him as the foremost poet of the Dutch screen, a perfectionist in a period when fine technique is often scorned. Set in Frisia in 1926, the film is a romantic's denunciation of hypocrisy; it is also a meditation on the extent of individual liberty amid the encroaching power of social convention. Angela

Nikolai van der Heyde (left) directing his comedy, HELP, THE DOCTOR'S DROWNING!

(Barbara Seagull), the American girl whose assertive, articulate brand of hedonism might have strayed from the present age, leads the shy young Harm Wouter from his bourgeois home for a journey through the countryside in search, Walden-like, of nature, freedom, and fulfilment. As does *Elvira Madigan,* it ends in catastrophe, but there is an irresistible poignancy in van der Heyde's style. Not merely the music of Georges Delerue, not just the exquisite clarity of Jörgen Persson's colour photography, but the very plangency of the conversations, the subtle use of long shots to isolate Harm and Angela in the fields of their liberty, the rustic groups and interiors that recall Ruysdael or Teniers—all constitute an appeal to the senses that is vital in a film so patently dedicated to Thoreau and the cause of youth.

Help, the Doctor's Drowning! (Help, de dokter verzuipt!, 1974), based on a popular novel, again shows van der Heyde as the miniaturist of the Dutch school, fostering the landscape and characters so beloved of his country's great painters. The film is a leisurely *divertissement,* somewhat in the Czech idiom, and reminiscent of Jirí Menzel's *Capricious Summer* in particular. The plot, set in the Twenties like that of *Angela,* is wafer-thin, and the charm and delicacy of the picture derive from the director's unselfish approach to his actors, letting them develop each role in their own manner and rhythm: the village doctor, the policeman, the builder, the parish priest. Van der Heyde takes a delight in the simple matters of bucolic life that evokes *Le déjeuner sur l'herbe,* and has a selective instinct for unrestrained comedy that makes his film entertaining from start to finish. At last there was a genuine *rapport* between film-maker and public in Holland; watching *Help, the Doctor's Drowning!* beside van der Heyde and his producer in a packed matinee theatre made one feel that things perhaps could not be quite the same again . . .

But Nikolai van der Heyde will never relinquish his dream: "The possibilities in film-making are boundless," he tells one. "You can look up at the sky, see a star, and bring it down in your hand."

C. FRANS WEISZ

Oh, Gods, how close are things
    that are and seem!
How like the dream is life, like
    life the dream!"
P.C. HOOFT (translated by
    Adriaan Barnouw)

If Nikolai van der Heyde appeared to be the Truffaut of the Dutch new wave, then Frans Weisz in his early phase seemed more in the mould of Rivette. Born of Hungarian and Dutch-Portuguese parentage, Weisz studied at the Netherlands Film Academy, and later at the Centro Sperimentale film school in Rome. In 1963, with Remco Campert, he made *Heroes in a Rocking Chair (Helden in een schommelstoel),* which starred Kitty Courbois and Graziella Polesinanti. At the age of twenty-six, he directed a brilliant short, *A Sunday on the Island of the Grande Jatte,* a Pirandellian exercise on the fascination of books that was imaginatively photographed by Gerard Vandenberg. The film's elegant compositions paid homage to the paintings of Seurat, but even more conspicuous were the fluency and ebullience of Weisz's technique. Such visual impressionism was abundantly developed in *Illusion Is a Gangster Girl (Het gangstermeisje,* 1967). The Italian impulse is strong, and Weisz's first feature is in sympathy with such contemporary directors as Bertolucci and Scavolini.

"Gangster Girl" is a phrase that tantalises the young writer, Wessel Franken; from it grows his novel, and when the book is about to be adapted into a movie, the demarcation lines between fiction and reality converge. Franken leaves his attractive wife in Amsterdam and travels south to write the script in Menton, and thence continues to Rome, where the fringes of fantasy at last roll back and compel him to break decisively with the image of the gangster moll that he simultaneously creates and destroys.

Franken's state of mind is mirrored lucidly in the film's fast-moving pattern of incidents. Premonitions of the future are outpaced by the action, by Franken's urgent need to express himself even if it means pulling apart from his wife—and only Widerberg could paint as deftly the bright moments of romance between these two in the train,

Still from Frans Weisz's A SUNDAY ON THE ISLAND OF THE GRANDE JATTE

or at home with their child. Franken is the vulnerable outsider, seeking in vain a code of behaviour *and* an ideal heroine, and rejecting the sterility and fastidiousness of the film's only steadfast marriage (a homosexual one). *Gangster Girl* is sophisticated and yet rarely mannered; it is rich in sub-plots and spurts of imagination that arouse only a temporary sense of confusion. Weisz's error is simply his own profound involvement in the movie, but he is still sufficiently gifted a director to give such personal preoccupations a universal currency.

Weisz has always regarded himself as a *metteur en scène* rather than an *auteur*. "If the phone rang now," he told me in the late Sixties, "and a producer asked me to direct a completed script with so and so in the leading parts, I'd accept." Like most of his friends and fellow graduates from the Film Academy, he was sceptical without being cynical. "People have been shouting 'crisis' since 1950, but now in 1968 there really is one. Distributors don't want to see Dutch films or screen them. For a long time the exhibitors and the Production Fund have been backing young directors, but now they see that there's no audience. So there is a reaction with a vengeance. We young film-makers can only cling in desperation to one another's mediocrity."

In 1969, Weisz attempted to recapture the enchanted mood of *Grande Jatte*. The result was a most agreeable comedy about the

Above: Kitty Courbois and Paolo Graziosi in ILLUSION IS A GANGSTER GIRL

Above: still from Weisz's MADE IN PARADISE

Creation. Called *Made in Paradise*—a title that hints accurately at the film's blend of innocence and irreverence—this short concerns an Adam and Eve who play noughts and crosses blithely in the sand, and gorge themselves with fruit, until the arrival of a third figure, "Robinson Crusoe," enlivens the atmosphere and subtly alters the relationship between the Original Lovers. Weisz's direction and the dialogue by Jan Vrijman combine to avoid the pitfalls of the subject, and the timing is neat. Adam, like all Weisz's characters, is unorthodox: a childlike nature beneath a middle-aged exterior, sucking his thumb at night and reacting sulkily rather than violently when Crusoe takes a fancy to his Eve.

* * *

We flash forward to 1978. Weisz is now one of the most successful makers of TV commercials in Holland. His wife, Astrid Weyman, who acted in *Gangster Girl,* and has edited all of Frans's pictures, is still involved in film and theatre. The lyricism and vaulting hopes of the earlier decade have dispersed, but Weisz has no quarrel with the fortunes of his career. *The Burglar (De inbreker,* 1972), and *Same Player Shoots Again (Naakt over de schutting,* 1973) effected a compromise with the realities of commercial film-making in the Netherlands. Both sported a likeable cast of actors, both were professionally shot and assembled, and both are forgettable comedy-thrillers. The multiscreen presentation that he directed for the Dutch pavilion at EXPO 70 in Osaka pointed the way towards a practical use of film, and Weisz now stoutly defends his absorption in the anonymity of TV spots. "There's a real art to the making of commercials," he maintains. Like the glass-blower whose creations are so numerous that there is no time for inspiration, merely craftsmanship, he works with zest and equanimity, secure in the knowledge that there is talent in reserve when he is once again permitted to embark on a topic close to his heart and mind.

D. PIM AND WIM

There is no question that modern Dutch cinema owes a considerable debt to Pim de la Parra and Wim Verstappen—or Pim and Wim, as they are affectionately known in film circles. These co-founders of the magazine "Skoop" were both graduates of the Netherlands Film Academy, and established their own company, Scorpio Films, in 1965. Together they created fifteen features in a dozen years, a prolific record unrivalled in Dutch cinema. Perhaps only three or four of these movies have any lasting value, but the impact of Pim and Wim on their contemporaries, and on the very system of production in the Netherlands, has been immensely significant. Besides, they have never worked *sub specie aeternitatis.*

Rudolf Lucieer in Verstappen's JOSZEF KATUS

Like all pioneers, they were patronised with derisory scorn for several years. They were the "young Turks" whose notion of shooting films with an English soundtrack was charming if hopelessly misguided; their early movies betrayed an adolescent's prurient vision of sex; and their productions were technically appalling. Financial success, however, is the key to recognition in the film world, and can eliminate such condescension in a night. When Pim's erotic suspense thriller, *Obsessions* (1968), starring Alexandra Stewart, and boasting an original score by Bernard Herrmann, found a ready market at home and was sold to sixty-four territories abroad, Scorpio came to be regarded with a measure of respect. *Blue Movie* (1970, no relation to Andy Warhol's production of the same name), directed by Wim, was an even more gigantic triumph at the box-office. Like Truffaut and Godard, Pim and Wim cherished a boundless affection for the American B film of the Forties and Fifties, and all their work was executed swiftly and dramatically, with one thrill piling on another and with even the most grotesque plot development glibly digested (*Blue Movie,* for instance, concerns a young man's inability to sustain an erection with the girl he loves).

During the twelve years of their partnership, Pim and Wim shared the duties of a film production team with unquenchable enthusiasm. Pim would direct one movie, with Wim as producer, and on the next assignment their roles might be reversed. To make their English dialogue more persuasive, they engaged the Scottish screenwriter, Charles Gormley, to collaborate on all their later scripts. No title was too outrageous for Scorpio, from *Heartbeat Fresco* to *VD* and *My Nights with Susan, Olga, Albert, Julie, Bill and Sandra*.

Ironically, while Pim and Wim placed survival before pretension, their most durable films sprang from their Dutch background and were spoken by Dutch actors and actresses in Dutch itself: *Joszef Katús, Frank & Eva Living Apart Together, Dakota, Alicia,* and *One People*. Nowhere else was the ingenuous spirit so effective as in *Katús* (full title: *The Not Too Happy Return of Joszef Katús to the Land of Rembrandt*), which was invited to the Critics' Week at Cannes in 1967. Many talented personalities began their career on this movie, including the cinematographers Jan de Bont and Wim van der Linden, and Nouchka van Brakel, later to become a director. Joszef Katús (Rudolf Lucieer) arrives in Holland on his birthday in April 1966. "He returned to Amsterdam to die," says the off-screen narration. He deposits his bag at the Central Station and visits a girlfriend named Mary. She is blonde and tender; there is something sacred about the way she embraces Katús, her white-stockinged legs floundering on the bed. Katús is obviously doomed. Verstappen has already shown, in a pre-credits sequence, how he will die, coughing blood in a foetal crouch, left to expire in the shabby streets like Michel in *A bout de souffle*. Katús makes the mistake of cheating an old acquaintance over a drugs deal, and he is perpetually followed by a menacing (but also risible) fellow in a dark coat. He has already abandoned one woman with an illegitimate child, he picks up another girl while buying some icecream, he deceives even Mary with a fraudulent cheque, and he is a somewhat flippant fellow-traveller where the Provo movement is concerned. Lucieer's performance, however, manages to render Katús in sympathetic terms as an essentially modest man betrayed by weakness rather than malevolence.

Who remembers the Provos now? They were the true ancestors of the students of May, 1968, and two years earlier in Holland they were publishing pamphlets opposing the marriage of Crown Princess Beatrix and Claus von Amsberg. They issued clandestine notes on how to make one's own explosives. They founded an alternative transport system by offering free bicycles, painted white, to the people of Amsterdam. Katús does not have the time or the inclination for commitment. "I'm in search of myself," he tells a TV interviewer, and later he comments: "I just want to *be*. That's much better than belonging to the Provos."

While *Joszef Katús* is concerned with the fate of an individual, its spasmodic, off-the-cuff style is a perfect reflection of the anxieties and uncertainties of that period, when an upheaval in Dutch society seemed possible, and idealism collided with tradition. Verstappen makes careless mistakes that would enrage the conventional Hollywood film crew. The fact that Mary wears a wedding ring on camera is, for instance, conveniently ignored. Sunlight spills repeatedly into the frame, often reducing the tonality to a milky grey. Pedestrians stare at the camera with embarrassing concern. The noise of passing aircraft drowns many an exterior conversation. The music of Aram Khachaturian threatens to shatter the primitive sound equipment. In 1978, though, one finds all this oddly sympathetic, rather as the character of Katús himself, for all his fickleness, still seems engaging. The very rudeness of the technique gives birth to a new dimension of realism. There is no doubt that *Joszef Katús* took place in Amsterdam in 1966; the Provo rallies were not staged. The film is wilfully coarse, but never artificial; banal, but never mendacious.

   Dakota (1974) again deals with the difficulty of retaining one's individuality in an emotionally restrictive world. Dick de Boer operates a private air cargo service in the Dutch West Indies. He accepts the occasional shady deal, but is suspicious when an attractive girl offers him $2,000 for a mere pleasure trip. It is the spur that sends him on a long and reckless flight to Europe in his ancient DC-3. *Dakota* survives on a minimum of dialogue. Dick's transatlantic journey

Willeke van Ammelrooy in ALICIA

forms the heart of the film, and all Verstappen's love for aircraft
emerges in a wordless mosaic of shots as the lonely pilot checks his
equipment and performs a hazardous refuelling process in mid-air.
Antoine Duhamel's music gives the adventure a dream-like quality,
and Kees Brusse does well to convey de Boer's affection for his plane
and the satisfaction he draws from his self-imposed solitude.

Alicia (1975), again directed by Verstappen, charts the rupture in
an urban marriage with remarkable restraint and lack of pretence,
and ends not in a sentimental reconciliation but on a note of
continuing dissatisfaction. Alicia (Willeke van Ammelrooy) has
learned that life beyond the four walls of her domesticity does not
have the champagne sparkle she had imagined; perhaps in conclusion she must acknowledge that her husband is far from perfect too,
as conscious of his own inadequacy as she is of hers. Verstappen's
gathering maturity as a director is indicated in the long opening
sequence, as he observes Alicia at home, taking a bath, gauging her
weight and her bodily charms, and almost subconsciously preparing
for flight. Apart from one hilarious interlude in which Pim de la Parra
tries to play the lecherous neighbour, the film is wrapped in quietness
and discretion. And finally it says more than many expensive American movies about the high price of admission commanded by modern
morality.

Pim de la Parra's successes as a director have been more modest. He
is primarily a catalyst, a centre of ceaseless energy and ideas for others
to put into practice. Two of his own movies, however, are more than
competent. *Frank and Eva, Living Apart Together* (1974) resounds with
Pim's puckish sense of humour and desire to shock, but its screenplay
contains a trenchant view of the permissive world, with Frank, the
libidinous, intemperate young car salesman, continually leaving his
beautiful mistress and returning on the double with his tail between
his legs. Using the bars and apartments of Amsterdam as his
locations, Pim communicates the reckless bravado assumed by society's parasites (and the contrast between fantasy and reality is wittily
underlined in the opening scene, when Frank's elaborate pretence at
suicide fails to deceive Eva). In the end, Frank is repulsed by his own
life-style and by the vulgar funeral given his old mentor Max; and he
and Eva cling together in a shrinking image that is as poignant in its
way as the last shot of *L'avventura*.

Returning to his roots in Surinam, Pim made his most satisfying
film, *One People* (*Wan pipel*) in 1976. The usual flippancy is repressed,
and Pim patently believes in the taut emotional situation of the
Surinamese—expected as he is to venture to the "home country"
(Holland) and yet also to remain loyal to the entrenched customs of
his native land. Roy (Borger Breeveld) is studying in Amsterdam and
is summoned home to attend his dying mother. While staying in
Paramaribo, he becomes infatuated with a Hindustani girl, and runs

Still from Pim de la Parra's ONE PEOPLE

headlong into the colony's racial barriers. His father, irascible, sententious, but never bitter, fights Roy's amorous ambitions. Eventually the young man's mistress from Amsterdam arrives by plane, and the film wanders to a sensible conclusion. *One People* treats a potentially explosive theme—racial intolerance—with warmth and good humour; it is a small film, but an honest one.

* * *

Pim and Wim, still good friends, have now decided to go their separate ways in the cinema. Wim has completed his first feature under a new banner. Entitled *Pastorale 1943,* it is founded on a novel by Simon Vestdijk about a small Dutch town during the Nazi Occupation. "It's a story," says Verstappen, "of people who have no experience in doing something against their government. They make every possible blunder." One eleven-minute scene shows a group of men discussing methods of killing a collaborator, but in fact he is the wrong person! "The Dutch do the wrong thing at the right time, and it is hard for them to recognise, even today, that not everyone was a hero during the war." With forty-two speaking parts, a budget of $600,000, and a famous book as its basis, *Pastorale 1943* hardly resembles the quickies shot by Pim and Wim in Scorpio days. *Pastorale 1943* is flecked with bright and dark patterns, and through its loosely-woven texture peeps a wry humour, the humour that sees the

A bungled reprisal against a local traitor in PASTORALE 1943

Dutch through life and that ensures their rejection of an authoritarian regime, whether it be their own or an invader's.

Most directors conceal, or repudiate their juvenilia; they like to come to a feature film as full-blown practitioners of their craft. Pim and Wim had the guts and the foolhardiness to make their mistakes in public. One loves them all the more for that.

E. ADRIAAN DITVOORST

The career of Adriaan Ditvoorst provides an acute commentary on the realities of Dutch film production. He has never had a commercial success, and he has not been compensated by critical applause outside the Netherlands. "Dutch film is like a little fire that's still burning," he told me with a sad smile some ten years ago. "Our pictures are too personal—but then that's natural. I'll be willing to make concessions to the box-office and to current trends, in my fourth or fifth feature, but not now." Today, he remains a sceptic. "If you need 700,000 guilders [approx. $300,000], you get 500,000 from the Production Fund, and in order to raise the balance, the producer compromises on the script that he shows to the distributor. Then, in debt to the distributor, he begins to influence the director . . ."

Ditvoorst is a Byronic figure, handsome and idéalistic, and forever on the brink of poverty. "I was born and raised a Catholic, that most

The soldier Oosterhuis and his girlfriend in THAT WAY TO MADRA

decadent and beautiful of religions." He lost his father when he was only fourteen; he had to leave school and work in an advertising agency to support his family. He joined the army and then persuaded a wealthy aunt to loan him enough money for classes at the Netherlands Film Academy, where he joined the famous "generation" of 1962-1964. During his last year there, he submitted his screenplay for *That Way to Madra (Ik kom wat later till Madra,* 1965), which stemmed from his military experiences. Salvador Dali has remarked that over the past six hundred years, artists have moved closer and closer to their subject, from medieval battle scenes to portraits, and have now gone *behind the eyes* of those they depict. Ditvoorst's work illustrates this theory perfectly. He marries wisps of reality and fantasy so smoothly that they become almost indistinguishable. Ordinary locations are rendered weird and unfamiliar by Ditvoorst's vision. Private Oosterhuis, summoned home to attend an ailing wife, never completes his journey. His most significant steps are into the past and future, a ferment of regrets and aspirations. Finally, Oosterhuis plunges back into actuality and we see the camera crew, the lights, etc. as he leaves the stage and resumes his life as a mere cipher in the Dutch army.

Ditvoorst's first feature, *Paranoia* (1967), based on a novel by W.F. Hermans, is a hermetic, sensual study of a paranoid youth, Arnold Cleever, who retreats from a disinterested Amsterdam into the circular logic of a nightmare, mistrusting everyone, even his faithful mistress, Anna, after a photo in the newspaper convinces his grasshopper mind that the authorities are searching for him. Ditvoorst constructs a haunting picture of the wintry city and of Cleever's acquaintances, so remote and grotesque that ultimately the boy seems like an island of sensitivity as he shoots his landlord with deliberate serenity. The last twenty minutes, when the film's centre of gravity shifts to Anna and her psychological disintegration (a reflection of Cleever's own collapse) are tightly interwoven and free of the irrelevant details that hamper the earlier narrative (although Ditvoorst revels in such *entr'actes,* a kind of *graffiti* in the margins of his movie). The soundtrack of *Paranoia,* like that of *Madra,* is riveting, with strange off-screen noises slapped disconcertingly against the images, and the music for organ, piano and guitar lending the film a dignity that belies its meagre budget of $40,000.

Ditvoorst's *Antenna* (1969) was an excursion into surrealism, filmed on location at the director's birthplace, Bergen-op-Zoom. "It was originally a strong story about the Provos," he recalls. "The Ministry of Culture rejected the idea, so two months later I submitted a script for a documentary about the carnival in Bergen. The cash was granted, and I immediately headed south and began shooting *Antenna!*" But the film is top heavy with pretensions. It consists of a series of totally unrelated incidents—a priest ogling a pubescent girl, the then fashionable actor, Pierre Clémenti, playing Christ and dispensing drugs like holy wafers to the hippies in "Paradiso," a café *cum* relaxation centre in Amsterdam, and an individual named Aquarius coming ashore on a raft loaded with such impedimenta as a jukebox and a lavatory bowl.

In 1972, Adriaan Ditvoorst fulfilled his promise with a fifty-minute

The blind boy in Ditvoorst's THE BLIND PHOTOGRAPHER

Left: *Kees van Eyck and Pamela Rose in PARANOIA. Right: "the cheerful neighbour" in THE CLOAK OF CHARITY*

featurette, *The Blind Photographer* (*De blinde fotograaf*). Based, like *Paranoia*, on a story by W.F. Hermans, it chronicles the bizarre adventure of a newspaper reporter who is assigned to profile a blind photographer. Jan de Bont's cinematography, luminous and sinister, tracks the reporter as he struggles blearily to work in the barren dawn, and then penetrates a curious household on the outskirts of the city. Here the photographer's parents greet him with suspicion and anticipation. Rejected temporarily, he strays into a nearby tavern, to be confronted first by an old man singing an aria in tune with an ancient 78 r.p.m. record, and then by a girl who, offended by her lover, blindfolds herself and staggers out into the street. Such moments are worthy of Polanski at his best, and when the journalist returns to talk with the photographer's mother, Ditvoorst swoops into some of the most moving sequences he has ever directed. The mother recalls, in bleached-out flashback, how she had saved with her son for his first camera. Later, the reporter enters the cavernous darkroom, where the blind photographer lurks like a wounded beast. "It's not that I can't see," he tells his visitor and victim, "but that I cannot *look*." Sightless eyes bulging, he strangles the reporter, an act of violence so logical in its absurdity that it may be construed as the successful outcome of a scientific experiment. The price of knowledge is death . . .

The world of these two creators, Hermans and Ditvoorst, has a cruel impermanence, a constant sense of the sand slipping precariously beneath the feet, and a heartfelt respect for hidden complexes. *Blind Photographer* is life viewed through the wrong end of a telescope, in sharp focus, yet beyond the reach of rational intervention.

Among Ditvoorst's favourite artists are Goya and Daumier; just as their drawings were their most notable accomplishments, so Ditvoorst's monochrome films have marked the high points of his *oeuvre*. He accepts that he must now work in colour to satisfy the demands of exhibitors and television companies, even if the visual effects are aggressive by comparison with black-and-white. *The Cloak of Charity (Der mantel der liefte,* 1978) is his most ambitious and decipherable movie, a piquant satire that vents all Ditvoorst's scorn for sexual, religious, and social hypocrisy. The guiding spirit on this occasion is not Polanski, but Buñuel.

F. PAUL VERHOEVEN AND ROB HOUWER

An habitual complaint in Dutch film circles is that the country is wanting in good producers. So many directors are forced to establish their own little companies in order to finance and market their films. During the Seventies, however, Rob Houwer has become a vital and influential figure. He has been damned with faint praise by the critics, but exhibitors—and the public—have responded with alacrity and enthusiasm to every film he has produced. Houwer himself began as a capable director, with shorts like *The Key (De sleutel,* 1963), and *Application (Aanmelding,* 1964), which won a Silver Bear in Berlin in 1964). He then set up camp in Munich, and sold an early Volker Schlöndorff social thriller, *A Degree of Murder (Mord und Totschlag)* to Universal for a reputed $75,000. Since then, he has taken calculated risks, invariably and courageously involving his own money, and has almost always repaid his loans to the Dutch Production Fund.

Houwer's major stream of triumphs began in 1971, when he became a partner in film-making with Paul Verhoeven. Their first release was a vivacious burlesque on the Amsterdam prostitution game, entitled *Business Is Business (Wat zien ik).* It succeeded where other Dutch films failed, purely because of its professional zest and abandon. *Turkish Delight (Turks fruit,* 1972), based on a novel by Jan Wolkers, was more ambitious, concealing a serious centre beneath a surface gloss of comedy and sexual misadventure. A lusty young sculptor falls in love with a nubile girl, only to discover that she is dying from a brain tumour. His encounters with the girl's parents, his cheerful vulgarity in the face of bourgeois conformity, and the consistently witty dialogue, help to make the film a whirlwind experience. What a far cry from Verhoeven's prize-winning short,

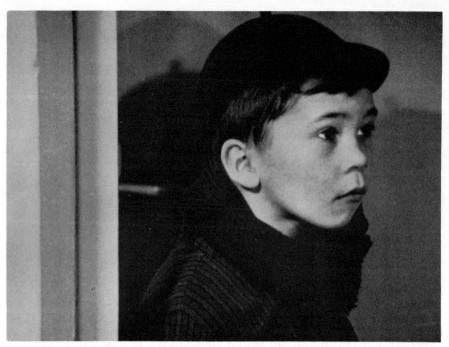

Still from Rob Houwer's early film, THE KEY

Party (*Feest*, 1963), in which a schoolboy finds his diffidence a handicap in appealing to a girl in another set; the situation could not have been treated with more unostentatious tact or sensitivity.

Less than three years after the international box-office acclaim for *Turkish Delight*, Verhoeven found himself able to flex his talents on a more robust tale: *Cathy Tippel* (*Keetje Tippel*, 1975), based on the novels by Neel Doff, a rich Belgian widow who wrote about her own turbulent exploits in Nineteenth-century Amsterdam. Verhoeven, with the aid of his regular scriptwriter, Gerard Soeteman, grasps the period atmosphere from the outset. The impoverished family migrating to the city from Friesland, sheltering in what might euphemistically be described as a hovel, flooded, cold, without food. Cathy's harsh experience as a washerwoman in a factory, where even her bread is pilfered. The coarseness of her sister, who demands the best tidbits because she, as a prostitute, earns the family's only pennies...

Although *Cathy Tippel* suffers from an inveterate emphasis on scatalogical detail, it is borne along by the splendid acting of Monique van de Ven, Rutger Hauer and others; and in Cathy's rise to luxury and some measure of prominence there is a universal optimism. Her pride helps her cope with life's capricious demands. One day she is tasting fine food and learning to ride, the next she is discarded by her lover and is embroiled in a political demonstration. "Money turns people into rats," she comments to a young benefactor, who eventually marries her and installs her in a country mansion.

Monique van der Ven in CATHY TIPPEL

The historical verisimilitude of *Cathy Tippel* was a tribute as much to Houwer and his team as it was to Soeteman and Verhoeven's meticulous research. *Soldier of Orange (Soldaat van Oranje,* later released by Rank as *Survival Run,* 1977) was an even more arduous undertaking, rendered doubly hazardous by the proximity of the drama to the hearts and memories of so many Dutch people. The film traces the story of Queen Wilhelmina's *aide-de-camp,* Erik Hazelhoff Roelfzema, from his student days in Leiden before the war to the emotional return to Holland at his monarch's side. Through the trials of this clumsy but engaging, and finally heroic, individual, Verhoeven describes a comprehensive picture of the Dutch at war—the air raids, the Jew-baiting, the viciousness of informers, the exploits of the Resistance—and he does so with a clever admixture of wit and cynicism. Hazelhoff's memoirs, and the film, recall "the supreme arrogance of a generation that greeted the catastrophic news, 'war!,' by serving a tennis ball."

Not many film-makers would have dared to show the anti-Jewish feelings that existed in Holland, or the quasi-Fascist initiation ceremonies among the university students in 1938, or the Dutch crowds pressing flowers into the hands of Nazi soldiers as they marched through the streets—an incident, says Verhoeven, that he based directly on newsreel footage. Against this courage must be set Verhoeven's lapses from taste (a couple copulating in sight of the Queen during her London exile, an SS lieutenant behaving like a comic-book caricature as he tries to stop Dutchmen taking ship for

Initiation ceremony at Leiden University in SOLDIER OF ORANGE/SURVIVAL RUN

England). Such vulgar moments are all the more obtrusive because so much of the film is achieved with discretion and economy. One cannot forget, for example, an execution in the dunes. The condemned man gazes round the windswept skyline while, faint in the background, there is the cry of a single bird . . . Or the convincing scenes filmed in England, with an assassination in Lincoln's Inn Fields perhaps the most gripping incident in the film.

Soldier of Orange was made at about the same time as the Joseph E. Levine/Richard Attenborough version of *A Bridge Too Far* was on location in Deventer, and on practically all counts, including pyrotechnics, the Houwer/Verhoeven epic outranks its rival. Verhoeven may be the butt of his intellectual contemporaries, and yet he has established a *rapport* with the Dutch public of which any director might be proud. He would like to work for television (one of his first successes was *Floris*, a kind of Dutch *Ivanhoe*, made as a series in 1968), and has his eye on Feuchtwanger's novel *Success*, which ends with the Nazi *Putsch* . . .

G. NOUCHKA VAN BRAKEL

It seems to be a rule-of-thumb that the number of film schools and their graduates expands in inverse proportion to the number of places available in the contracting cinema industry. In Holland, the problem has been as acute as it has anywhere else. Many keen young students of the Netherlands Film Academy have been unable to proceed to full-scale work. Nouchka van Brakel has followed a sagacious route, starting her career as assistant on—and actress in—*Joszef Katús,* and then venturing into short films. *Sabotage* (1967) won praise for its insight into the relationship between children and grown-ups, and *Baby in the Tree* (1969) is a signal achievement by any standards. Feathery light in treatment, the film observes three young boys who are left to mind a small baby in her pram on a languid summer's afternoon in Amsterdam. The escapades, the aggressive faces, the improvised dialogue, the pleasant scenery, all work to the advantage of this most delightful movie, as unsentimental as *Hugo and Josefin* and as technically polished as *Skater-Dater.*

Throughout the late Sixties, Nouchka maintained her involvement in the Dutch film scene, as well as teaching in schools. She was scriptgirl, for instance, on Adriaan Ditvoorst's *Antenna,* and she played a role in Wim Verstappen's *Festival of Love,* a thirty-minute melodrama about an affair and a *crime passionel* on the film festival circuit. Her own bent inclined towards educational issues and the

Marina de Graaf in Nouchka van Brakel's THE DEBUT

tribulations of old folk. *One Has To Go On Looking (Het blijft zoeken,* 1971) was made for television, and deals with a divorcee and her teenage daughter who is set on leaving home. *Ageing (Ouder worden,* 1975) is a benevolent, discerning documentary about the reality and implications of growing old: the physical infirmity, the surfeit of spare time, the solitude that, in youth so coveted, develops into loneliness. "Every seven years, I'd like to make a film about ageing," says Nouchka.

As plain reportage is often a discipline for the incipient novelist, so documentaries may, for the young director, be a rewarding antecedent to more imaginative films. Nouchka van Brakel was already in her thirties when she found the opportunity to make a fictional movie. Her episode in the portmanteau production, *Melancholy Tales (Zwaar moedige verhalen voor bij de centrale verwarming,* 1975), is much the most intriguing of the four stories, all drawn from a collection by Heere Heeresma, a very popular Dutch writer of the moment. On a windswept, rainy day, beside an endless canal, a local shopkeeper asks the passing mailman for a light. From such banal, innocuous beginnings, this tale develops into an eerie exercise in suspense, worthy of Bergman or Poe. The mailman, glimpsed first as he swoops towards the camera with black hat and cloak sinister against the fading sky, becomes an embodiment of Death. With charm and guile he ensnares his victim. His victory won, however, he is magnanimous, sheltering the shopkeeper with his cloak as he rows their boat faster and faster up the Lethe-like canal, towards a lurid sunset.

The Début (Het debuut, 1977) is Nouchka's first full-length film, and a confident justification of her belief that a woman can render her sex much more precisely on screen than a male director can (save, perhaps, for her idol, Howard Hawks). "I had always dreamed of making a feature," she says. "Dutch documentaries had relied too much on observation from the outside. I wanted to show *emotions.*" Caroline is a child of our time, a teenage tomboy whose set, knowing face conceals her essential vulnerability. She watches the emotional hiccups of her elders with detachment and studied cynicism. When Hugo, a middle-aged friend of her parents, returns to Holland with his wife after an overseas assignment, he is quickly beguiled by Caroline's *esprit.* The more flippantly she behaves, the more she compromises him, the likelier Hugo is to plunge into an affair with her. Nouchka does not view this hectic relationship with the mischievous eye of Nabokov; she knows the wisdom of wit—"Hooray, I've lost my virginity!" yells Caroline from her hotel balcony after her first night with Hugo—and in such moments one regards the girl, rather than the man, as victim of the situation. Inevitably, the euphoric zest of the affair deteriorates, symbolised by a furtive weekend at a bleak coastal resort. Hugo is impatient with her childish ways, and she in turn resents his peevish behaviour at a discotheque.

Almost on the rebound, she finds herself attracted to a boy of her own generation, and is shattered when he takes advantage of her pliancy.

Caroline may shout at Hugo that she no longer loves him, but when she joins her parents at the airport to say farewell to her ex-lover and his wife, she dashes impetuously through the departure gate for one last hug. "That daughter of yours will never grow up," says her father to his wife, and only we, the audience, wince at the emotional irony of the remark. Parents, as Jan Vrijman also suggests in his *Girl of Thirteen* (1974), are too preoccupied to heed the quickening of young emotions.

Nouchka van Brakel conveys the pain of youth's first disabusement, with greater sensitivity than any Dutch director apart from René van Nie. If she fails at all, it is in reconciling the conflicting expectations of older man and younger woman; the balance of our sympathy soon tilts towards the more expressive Caroline. When Hugo weeps with distress behind the wheel of his car, the windscreen is more than a physical barrier, it divides us from this unfortunate man whose dilemma seems faintly embarrassing.

H. JOS STELLING

The autodidact, so common a figure in musical history, is rarely found in the cinema. John Cassavetes is one such personality; Kevin Brownlow and Werner Herzog are others. Like them, Jos Stelling has taught himself the rudiments, and something of the art, of the cinema, and will gladly devote years of his life to projects in which he believes. He was only thirty when his first feature, *Mariken van Nieumeghen* (1974) participated in competition in Cannes. The film had devoured eight years, and the least one can say about Stelling's work is that it vouches for his meticulous historical research. The Middle Ages intrigue him, and both *Mariken* and its successor, *Everyman* (*Elckerlyc*, 1975) are set in that period when, as Hobbes declared, life was "nasty, brutish, and short." Mariken is a young girl who is gradually corrupted by the age's desperate hedonism in the face of an all-consuming plague, and falls victim to the Devil. The film is steeped in blood and sex, but the effect is overpowering. There is no restraint in Stelling's depiction of lust and death. He is obviously aspiring to the achievement of *The Seventh Seal* (there is even a masque that brings the Bergman film to mind) and to the tradition of Bosch, but the impact is as crude as that of a Roger Corman movie. Working mainly at weekends, Stelling used some six hundred players. No professional actors were involved. *Elckerlyc*, a medieval morality play, is more modest in conception and execution. It was shot in a Thirteenth-century castle in Ghent in Belgium, over a period of three weeks. Again the cast consisted entirely of amateurs.

Rembrandt fecit 1669, Stelling's latest work, represents a dramatic advance and is a triumphant vindication of his particular approach to historical cinema. In the manner of the Straubs' *Chronicle of Anna Magdalena Bach,* the film recounts the life of Rembrandt year by year, incident after incident. Any director dealing with Rembrandt is bound to be caught up in an overwhelming struggle with the beauty of the paintings themselves. Stelling "re-creates" some of the most famous pictures—"The Anatomy Lesson" and "The Nightwatch"— but he concentrates primarily on Rembrandt's emotional reactions to the pain and trials that life condemns him to endure: the disillusionment of Saskia's death, the humiliation of his bankruptcy hearing, the demise of Titus... Quizzical, puckish, ironic, wistful, the painter gazes into the camera as he prepares each new self-portrait. Towards the end, as Rembrandt paints like one in a state of grace, beyond anguish and bitterness, Stelling shows how Rembrandt was always alert to that flowering of inner consciousness that in most men lies dormant until the tranquillity of their declining years.

The surprising aspect of *Rembrandt fecit 1669* is not the uncanny sense of period, for Stelling's previous work had established him as a small master in this field, so much as the Bressonian rigour of the film. Sequence after sequence is played out in virtual silence, so that a sound effect like the wind rustling the leaves over Titus's grave is doubly potent. The turbulence of *Mariken* is banished from these

Ton de Koff as the ageing Rembrandt in REMBRANDT FECIT 1669

quiet, lofty rooms where Rembrandt, a fugitive from his contemporary world, lurks behind doors and curtains, his face like a half-moon contemplating his rue. Frans Stelling (the director's brother) plays the young Rembrandt, Ton de Koff the painter in old age. Neither man portrays Rembrandt as a national saint; his selfishness and callous treatment of Saskia, and then of Geertje Dirkx and Hendrickje Stoffels, are gravely underlined. Charles Laughton may have achieved the most sympathetic of screen Rembrandts, and Bert Haanstra's documentary may come closest to the meaning of the man's *oeuvre*, but Stelling's film is unlikely to be surpassed as a synthesis of fact and feeling.

I. ERIK VAN ZUYLEN

The effect of the Second World War on Holland has been analysed by various film-makers. Most of them, however, have avoided the psychological issues. Erik van Zuylen, in *The Last Train (De laatste trein,* 1975) depicts a family that has been blown off course by the events of the Occupation. The father, Anton Karn, has operated the same signal-box all his life, and on this remote stretch of line in southern Holland, his wife provokes a catastrophe in which many folk are injured, and disappears with a German officer. Eight years later the landscape is unchanged. The passing trains hurl their refuse over the garden patch beside the signal-box. The local people seek money as

Still from Erik van Zuylen's THE LAST TRAIN

ravenously as the dike rats devour the soil beneath the ballast way. Karn's sons peddle old magazines for a spot of extra cash; a girl makes pennies by lifting her skirt before the snotty gaze of neighbouring children; a cripple, clearly a victim of the same shameful past, sells cigarettes from a bike-chair. In van Zuylen's eyes, this grotesque, introverted community is a paradigm for Holland in the aftermath of war. Virulent hatred runs just below the surface of daily routine, and the family's resentment stands united against the Dutch army; instead of "rebuilding" Holland, the soldiers plod along, scavenging, even raping, whenever the opportunity arises. The details of this lugubrious film matter more than its ungainly, distended shape. One remembers the ambivalent smile the mother gives to her German lover as he marches past with his men, or the father's sudden jerk into wakefulness after sleeping impassively through an alarm clock and other summonses, or the moment when Lois discovers a picture of her vanished mother in a decrepit hamper filled with white rats.

Van Zuylen recently completed a 40-minute TV film entitled *The Wimshurst Machine* (*De elektriseermachine van Wimshurst*), taken from a novel by W. F. Hermans about a man who recalls his lost youth and his passion for strange contraptions.

J. JACOB BIJL

For a generation entering the cinema during the Seventies, the French new wave is already receding over the horizon into history. Other influences come into play. Jacob Bijl, for example, obviously admires the work of Bergman, and his *Scrim* (1976) is an overt, if also perceptive, *hommage* to *Persona*. His first film, *Jealousy* (*Zwartziek*, 1974), was made for TV, and revealed him as a gifted director in the Cassavetes mould. *Jealousy* was improvised from beginning to end, although the acting is so skilful and impassioned that hesitations and repetitions are hardly noticeable. A draughtsman and his wife find that their relationship is starting to crumble. The girl (played by Jessamin Stärcke, Bijl's wife) has an impromptu affair with a stranger, and this brings matters to a head. The conversations and the domestic arguments are persuasive throughout, and the empty, pluvious countryside reflects the hopelessness of the marriage.

*Scrim** is chamber cinema at its most hermetic. Maria (Jessamin Stärcke) is a photographer, visiting the city where her former lover, Jim, has been living. When she arrives at his apartment, she encounters another girl, closely resembling herself, named Ann (Geraldine Chaplin), who claims to be Jim's wife. The film opens with Maria's ringing the doorbell, and then disappearing into the dark well of the house entrance. Apart from a couple of scenes in the local prison, where Jim and Ann meet, the remainder of *Scrim* is played out

*"Scrim = a flag which is made of transparent material. Its effect is partly to cut off, partly to diffuse, the source of light" (*Cut!-Print!*, New York, 1972)

Geraldine Chaplin in Jacob Bijl's SCRIM

in the small apartment. Both women are uneasy. Ann is nervous and overwrought, suspicious of Maria, and emotionally enmeshed by her rival's memorabilia that comes to light in the apartment—the photos on the walls, the big stone Maria and Jim found while on holiday in Rome . . . In a fish tank, water lizards prowl, amphibian replicas of the human rivals who observe them curiously through the glass. Like these salamanders, Ann and Maria change their colours, blend their personalities, grope towards each other with ambiguous glances and faltering, half-completed comments.

Scrim is a movie about waiting, touching, experimenting. Bijl's pastiche of *Persona* is complete when Ann and Maria watch a cold-blooded Nazi massacre from a war film on TV, and when Ann burns the photographs taken of her by Maria. The significance of the film, however, lies in Bijl's ability to sustain a mood and to direct actresses. There are also one or two brilliant cinematic contrivances: when, for instance, Ann rings the bell to enable her to leave prison after visiting Jim, the door is opened by a guard and the girl seems to go *into* captivity, rather than *out* into a free world.

K. HERBERT CÜRIEL

Hugo Claus, the Belgian novelist, has been the source of several Dutch films during the past decade. *Year of the Cancer (Het jaar van de Kreeft,* 1975) focuses, like much of his work, on the ever-maturing role

Rutger Hauer and Willeke van Ammelrooy in YEAR OF THE CANCER

of women in modern society, a development before which men retreat in confusion, proving themselves in the process as stringent prisoners of their sex as ever any woman has been. A hectic love affair mates Toni (Willeke van Ammelrooy), a hairdresser, and Pierre (Rutger Hauer), a conservative businessman. He is financially comfortable, and responds to the earthy non-conformism of his new partner. She is beyond the first heedless flush of youth, and yearns for an orthodox life. But the infatuation dies swiftly. The thrill of discovering each other physically is succeeded by the process of living and squabbling in unison. Toni feels incongruous in smart restaurants, and begins to despise Pierre's bourgeois sensibilities. Her insecurity bobs to the surface and she returns to her former "husband," aware, perhaps, that in so doing she bows before convention as much as if she had married Pierre. Herbert Cüriel's direction in his first feature (since *The Activist*, a political movie) is impressive. The dialogue is salty and the love scenes, usually so prone to *cliché*, are warm and unashamed. *Year of the Cancer*, produced by the enterprising George Sluizer, is among the few Dutch movies inexplicably neglected by foreign distributors.

8. OFF THE BEATEN TRACK

A RENE VAN NIE

"Because we have such a small film industry in Holland, you have to
do a great deal yourself—you must keep the rhythm going, a feature
every year or eighteen months if possible." For René van Nie, it is the
loss of creative energy, rather than Time, that is the "wingèd chariot
hurrying near." He comes from a miner's family on the Belgian
border. When he was twelve, he could have entered the pits and
learned the trade. But René did not want to be a miner, and by his
mid-teens he was in Amsterdam, living alone in an apartment and
acting as a pimp for American soldiers. With the proceeds, he
attended art school in the evenings. At sixteen he resolved to enter the
film industry, but his first post, as assistant cameraman to Max de
Haas, came through sheer chance. He was interviewed nine times by
de Haas before he was offered the job. De Haas was at that time
shooting newsreel footage in the Low Countries for the British,
Canadians, and Australians. René covered all manner of incidents,
from meat strikes to the case of a girl with a radioactive needle
implanted in her head! It was a hectic and valuable apprenticeship.

He worked subsequently at Cinecentrum in Hilversum, specialis-
ing in documentaries. *Holland* (1968), directed for the Eurovision
network, remains a brilliantly unorthodox study. The commentary,
by Jan Blokker, avoids the habitual phrases, teaming up with the
imagery to break down one's preconceptions of the country, and
drawing attention to the Calvinism that still colours Dutch life more
than dikes or tulips do. *Bronbeek for Example* (*Bronbeek bijvoorbeeld*,
1969) infuriated the authorities with its outspoken portrait of an old
soldiers' home, and reminds one strongly of Franju's short, *Hôtel des
Invalides.*

René van Nie soon abandoned television. "Budgets are too tight,"
he says, "and it's difficult to do an original film." In 1975, he released
his second feature*, *Anna, Child of the Daffodils* (*Kind van de zon*), which
proves how smoothly and audaciously he has seized on the complex
potentialities of modern cinema. He and his co-writer, Jonne Severijn
(himself no mean documentarist) have organised the narrative in two
parallel currents of thought, flowing alongside each other, yet in
opposing directions. This format affords the ideal counterpoint for

---

*The first, *Five on the Four Days' Race,* was a commercial success but a comedy outside
the mainstream of van Nie's development.

Josée Ruiter in ANNA, CHILD OF THE DAFFODILS

the story of a young girl recovering from schizophrenia. Various incidents and pressures that led to her illness are seen in different perspectives. Anna is typical of a generation that has been offered more emotional freedom than it can assimilate, and it is to the film's credit that all the characters—Anna, the bourgeois parents, her sister, her brother—appear sensitive and sympathetic, whereas the personalities in Ken Loach's comparable *Family Life* are painted in all too black and white terms. The acting, particularly by Josée Ruiter, is admirable, and in *Anna* there are few of the technical asperities that usually mar Dutch features. It is an ambitious work, written and directed with absolute control and conviction, even if its elaborate mechanism may puzzle the impatient viewer.

René's third ·major film, *A Silent Love* (*Een stille liefde*, 1977) was constructed in much more comprehensible, linear terms, and nevertheless failed at the box-office. The approach is emotional rather than analytical. The collapse of a marriage is one of the most painful and embarrassing spectacles of the modern world. In *A Silent Love*, a young boy, Sem, is taken without permission from school by his father, who has already lived apart from his wife for six months. As they travel south through Belgium, father and son gradually forge a new, if infinitely precarious, relationship. Twice the boy determines to return to his school and the daily round he equates with security. Again and again the father mends the situation with desperate

Sem de Jong and Cor van Rijn in A SILENT LOVE

appeals; he confides in Sem, telling him about the "other woman" who had caused the divorce. When at last he bows to the inevitable, and returns Sem to his estranged wife, he has grown a little in our estimation. The two parents stare at each other helplessly, much moved, and then the father walks away disconsolately towards the waiting police car. One of the film's many ironies is that Sem's mother lodges an official complaint against her husband ànd, when she begins to recognise the man's genuine need for his son's company, finds that the police cannot annul it.

The brief, final confrontation between husband and wife is the nearest van Nie permits one to come to the relationship, and yet, through skilful suggestion in dialogue and behaviour, he has amply demonstrated the impossibility of this marriage. Cor vàn Rijn gives a marvellously vulnerable performance as the husband; brittle by nature, humourless (especially when trying to manage a horse!), and impulsive, he seeks in Sem the kind of understanding and maternal affection that the boy, with the best will in the world, simply cannot offer him.

"All my films are about human beings and their relations to one another," says René, as he prepares his next feature, *A Deadly Sin*. "My subjects are international. Audiences in Poland loved *Anna,* and in Moscow people wept after the festival screening of *A Silent Love*." René van Nie, like many of the world's foremost film-makers, is a solitary and extremely tender man, whose apparent self-confidence is a prophylactic against the despair and pathos of human kinship.

B. JOHAN VAN DER KEUKEN

There is a perpetual dialectic in the films of Johan van der Keuken. The emotions of the moment are in conflict with the detachment of the human mind as it regards people and situations. Van der Keuken's *avant-garde* work comprises documentaries and the occasional fantasy that somehow reorganises the everyday into the imaginary. All are visual analogues for the verbal debate of pamphlet or seminar. His career burgeoned during the Sixties, when he made several striking programmes for VPRO television (see Chapter Ten); but although he became well-known to intelligent viewers, he remained an artistic recluse, constantly reassessing his style and approach. As Dr. H.S. Visscher, author of a monograph on van der Keuken, writes: "For a while, you think you understand exactly what he's saying and showing and then suddenly you realise you have landed in the realm of the unknown."[6]

Blind Child (*Blind kind,* 1964) is van der Keuken's first notable achievement. It observes, like a profoundly sympathetic voyeur, the tribulations of the blind. Youngsters are seen alone, surrounded by natural bird sounds, but lurching about, uncertain of the space they

BEAUTY (and, reflected in the glasses, the director, Johan van der Keuken)

inhabit. Some shots, such as those showing children caressing pigeons, are unequivocally moving. Others, like the subjective collision of a blind youth with a lamp-post, communicate the pain and humiliation that attend the handicapped. The sequel, *Herman Slobbe* (*Blind kind 2*, 1966), brings the individual blind youth into contact with the adult world, and with politics in the widest sense of the word. Slobbe, at fourteen, quivers with resentment, brushing aside any attempt by the film-maker to pity him or to identify with his exasperation. Slobbe wants the freedom to take his own decisions, and his conversation is laced with hatred for an older generation in whose drabness he senses his own scarifying future.

Van der Keuken's journey of self-discovery through film led him steadily towards a disintegration of narrative line. *A Film for Lucebert* (*Film voor Lucebert,* 1967) explores the attitudes and accomplishments of a modern Dutch painter and poet. Lucebert's canvases and collages are savagely primary in their use of colour. Van der Keuken inserts his own live images to give the paintings a three-dimensional presence. Pigs' snouts in the marketplace, crabs, painted pebbles on a beach, an emaciated woman hawking bunches of heather: these sights expand within the spectator, like stones dropped into the waters of the mind.

In *Beauty* (1970, van der Keuken stresses the artificial character of our existence. Every shot is deliberately false: "A documentary on fakes," as the director himself terms it. The black protagonist of

Scene from van der Keuken's DIARY

Beauty has to transform himself with makeup powder before he can function in the role of the white man he simultaneously apes and reviles. Max Ernst and René Magritte are influences on this movie which, without van der Keuken beside one to elucidate its theory, appears pretentious and wilfully obscure.

Diary (1972) is suddenly much more coherent, marking the start of a new and altogether more confident phase in van der Keuken's career. Filmed in Amsterdam and Africa while the director was awaiting the arrival of his wife's child, *Diary* makes one aware of the fragile, irredeemable qualities of life and at the same time of the problems that increasing population awakens in the Third World. As a contrast between the affluent society of the West and the primitive labour community of Africa, the film is effective *agit-prop*. Van der Keuken does not strike blindly at his targets. He modulates the pace of *Diary* with the utmost care, and many of his sharpest barbs are delivered through a subtle combination of image and subtitle. *The Reading Lesson (Het leesplankje*, 1973) contemplates Dutch education and its relevance to events outside the classroom. In certain Dutch schools, children are given news of the *coup d'état* in Chile and other international developments. Van der Keuken's skill, as always, is in the establishment of a dialectic—this time between the traditional introduction to reading, via pictures and comics, and the realities of the contemporary world.

Few Dutch directors have travelled so extensively in search of their material as van der Keuken has during the Seventies. "For each film," he told me, "my outline consists of only a few pages. Instead of a script I opt for a list of items, so that I can strike out some and replace them with others. It's a way of remaining open to fresh ideas and metaphors." *The New Ice-Age (De nieuwe ijstijd*, 1974) analyses the effect of poverty in Groningen in the Netherlands, and in the mountain villages of Peru. The Inca Indians are addicted to cocoa leaves and in thrall to the United States by virtue of their minerals. The Dutch family in northern Holland work in an icecream factory, slaves to excruciating monotony. *The Palestinians* (1975) again deals in contrasts, focusing on people along the Israeli-Lebanese border. A recently completed documentary on the Waddenzee region, between the Dutch coast and the northern islands, describes the different layers of activity, biological, political, and economic. The preservation of nature cannot be just a hobby; it has powerful economic and social consequences for these Dutch folk.

One can dispute neither the lucidity of Johan van der Keuken's vision nor the even-tempered rationalism of his political ideals. He is as indispensable to the landscape of Dutch cinema as Chris Marker is to the French; at his best when dealing with individual human pain rather than with ethical abstractions; and diminished only by his unwavering seriousness of exposition.

Still from Louis van Gasteren's STRANDING

C. LOUIS A. VAN GASTEREN

The most flamboyant and volatile of the independent Dutch film-makers remains Louis A. van Gasteren. Brought up in a theatrical family (his father was a renowned actor, his mother a singer), he joined a newsreel organisation and began writing screenplays as a young man. In 1950, he founded his own company, Spectrum Films, and although he did make a lively documentary about chocolate for Van Houten, he has firmly rejected commercial work since. He uses naught but his own equipment and is an ardent admirer of the American experimental film-makers, as well as of Antonioni and Resnais. His ambitious, half-hour work, *The House* (*De huis,* 1962) is an attempt to split up a fragment of thought in time. Thus it flashes back and forth throughout the history of an old house that is in the process of being demolished. Memories of love, of birth, and of death in the war, are revived. In the words of van Gasteren, "As the house is pulled down, so the lives of its occupants are constructed, not out of a need to put everything into chronological order, but from the knowledge of the inevitable end."

As long ago as the mid-Fifties, van Gasteren made a thriller based on a real-life incident, the grounding of a passenger liner on a sandbank off the Dutch coast. Location shots of the stricken vessel were intercut with studio sequences involving some skullduggery worthy of *Journey into Fear.* A fortune in uncut diamonds is aboard the

Still from van Gasteren's THE HOUSE, produced for his own company, Spectrum Film

ship, and in a race against time two rival groups try to recover the trunk containing the gems. *The Stranding* (*Stranding, SOS Ecuador*, 1956), although competently acted and put together, is itself stranded in the past, its dark assignations reminiscent of nothing so much as Carné's melodramas of an earlier decade.

This ebullient director is bursting with ideas covering every subject from germ warfare to higher mathematics. (The fact that van Gasteren owns a *house-cum-studio* in central Amsterdam is typical of the almost pugnacious desire for self-sufficiency inherent in the Dutch. Instead of agents, one discovers, many directors have their own offices and secretaries. John Ferno, when he lived in the Netherlands, ran his affairs from a windmill used by the Dutch Resistance during the war.)

In 1970, van Gasteren completed a chilling documentary about a former inmate of Belsen, who is liberated of his subconscious burden of terror by undergoing doses of LSD, and "confessing" to a Professor of Psychiatry at Leiden University. *Do You Get It Now Why I'm Crying?* is filmed soberly and realistically, and for the most part resists the temptation to flash back to gruesome images of the concentration camps. It sounds phoney and fabricated; but as this elderly man talks quietly in a white-walled consulting room, his fears are suddenly *there* on the screen, in a remarkably abstract form.

Fascinated by the title of that film, van Gasteren embarked on a

series of shorts called *Do You Get It?* In the third of these experiments
in perception, the director lectures his audience about people's
response to a camera. A brief scene, showing a policeman on traffic
duty and a street cleaner who seized his chance to be on TV, is
repeatedly scrutinised by van Gasteren. Such films, although
pedagogic in tone, reveal the cogency and analytical cast of the
director's mind. Sadly, van Gasteren has never been able to release a
full-length feature film. *There Is No Train for Zagreb*, which was years in
gestation, and finally languished, was intended as a non-stop series of
impressions. Language is seen as a limitation, a circle of constriction.
Van Gasteren intended it to be a sequel to *The House*, examining the
various planes of time. Yet this same director, who has written a book
on Marshall McLuhan and started a Foundation for the investigation
of art and technology, was also able to produce a harrowing
documentary on the Biafran struggle for independence. He shot it in
five days and nights and edited it for 120 hours with Johan van der
Keuken. The film was widely acclaimed, and was screened in the
United States and Canada.

Similarly, van Gasteren turned his TV programme, *Je ne sais pas. . .
Moi non plus* (1973) from what might so easily have been a boring
interview into a painfully honest and inspiring encounter with an
elderly woman in an impoverished French farming community. At
his best, van Gasteren fulfils the first duty of an artist: he *reaches* his
audience. It is hardly his fault is that communication is so honest, so
abrasive, that one winces, and turns away.

D. FRANS ZWARTJES

The "underground" cinema has never spread deep roots in the stern
religious earth of Holland. Political documentaries are one thing;
sexual perversion and surrealism are quite another. Frans Zwartjes, a
mild man who at first worked completely outside the subsidised
system, is the exception who proves the rule. His style is obsessive, and
instantly recognisable. His girls are creatures of the night, their faces
harshly lit so that lips gleam like black welts against the white cheeks,
reminiscent of Japanese *kabuki* players. In *Birds* (1969), one of
Zwartjes's favourite actresses, Trix (who also happens to be his wife),
lies with legs splayed on a couch. She dangles, like a child its yoyo, a
paper bird on the end of a piece of string. The camera slides and rocks
as though hypnotised, and the white shape, fluttering to the raucous
accompaniment of feral squeaks off-screen, and set against the girl's
impassive face, becomes the vehicle—perhaps the fetish—of her
sexual hunger. In *Seats Two* (1970), Trix and Moniek act out a Lesbian
interlude on a couch. Trix looks through sunglasses at a photograph
of some obscure mountain landscape, while Moniek picks her nose
desultorily. The physical attraction between the women is almost

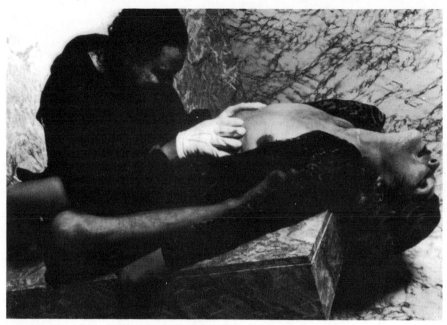

Still from Zwartjes's CONTACT

tangible—stockinged legs inclined to one another, touching and retreating, stretching and stroking.

Zwartjes's is an hermetic world of guilt, disgust, and defilement. In *Home Sweet Home* (1970), a haughty couple enact an erotic ritual worthy of Buñuel. The man wears white gloves and tries furiously to rouse his mate by thrusting a beetle into her face. Like a climax, she rises to her knees, extends a shiny-shod leg, and crushes the creature into the pillow. All this is related in a jolting sequence of images, with Zwartjes cutting against the beat, and giving thereby a palpable visual charge to the climate of sexual hesitancy and oppression. It's hardly surprising when the couple disappear beneath the bed like the necrophiliac nobleman in *Belle de Jour*.

A musician and violin-maker by training, Zwartjes takes great pains over his sound effects. Feelings are denoted by sounds. In *Eating* (1969), loud clock-ticking alternates ceaselessly with a four-note clarion call, while the camera records a kinky "eat-in" with three bare-bosomed girls, one wearing a hirsute male mask, tasting food that is simultaneously scalding and aphrodisiac, and eventually plastering one another with sauce and pie. The effect is grotesque, as though a primitive urge were being gratified, the debasement bringing its own self-transcendence.

Living (1971), like much of Zwartjes's work, takes place in the film-maker's own home. He and Trix prowl from room to room in a ritualistic trance. He, nervous, fastidious, and immaculately dressed, never touches his partner; but sex, like a thief in the night, is unmistakably present. The film is a virtuoso exercise, photographed entirely by Zwartjes himself with a hand-held camera kept miraculously out of sight. The wide-angle lens creates a vertiginous impression. Walls reel. Trix's legs loom like skyscrapers. The house appears to encase these troubled lovers, as they walk through the heavy water of their dream, higher and higher, until the skylight offers an escape to light and—perhaps—reality.

Zwartjes's two visions of womanhood in *Behind Your Walls* (1970) have the febrile frustration associated with his earlier work. A torpid heat reduces movement to fidgets and hesitations. But in *Through the Garden* (1971), the longing for freedom finds expression. Zwartjes breaks out, like a submariner surfacing, from his interior fantasies, to conclude on a note of liberation, as he and his family scamper round his orchard in accelerated motion as if, in Méliès fashion, they were discovering the cinema for the first time and communicating their joy in vivid filmic terms.

Contact (1974), one of Zwartjes's longest and most ambitious films, has three parts. In the first, Lodewijk lies asleep like Caligari's Cesare on a marble slab, his hands encased in white gloves. Some inner call rouses him from his trance, and he embraces a girl in a leopardskin. During the act of love, their limbs crawl and creep rather than move normally. There is a solemnity about this performance that is concluded when Lodewijk relapses into sleep, his hands clasped as if

Willeke van Ammelrooy in Frans Zwartjes's IT'S ME

in death across his waist. In the second part, a man and a girl explore each other, in close-up. Each gesture is tentative, as if afraid of acknowledging the basic animal drive; and in the last section of *Contact* the engulfing rooms and stairways of the Zwartjes home again predominate. Jerking, pumping water sounds fill the soundtrack as a girl with a cigarette dangling from her mouth, and Zwartjes himself, observe and harass a victim—a bearded individual who tries to find a corner in which to sleep. In the end, as a clock chimes ominously, the intruder—still swathed in bedclothes—is dragged down the final flight of stairs. There is a horrible resonance about this final image. The stairwell becomes a Stygian abyss, and the smooth, sliding movement of the man's descent, drawn by an unseen power, suggest the impotence of the dreamer.

Sex for Zwartjes is a ceremony in which decorum only just gets the better of brutality. In *It's Me* (1976), which runs for 68 minutes, there is no overt eroticism, but the whole film is bathed in a sensual laminate of desire. An actress receives a proposal (or a proposition?) over the telephone. One cannot hear what is at stake; one knows only that her decision is vital, and for the next hour or so the camera follows Willeke van Ammelrooy relentlessly around her tiny apartment. Makeup in Zwartjes's world constitutes both a mask and a form of imprisonment. Willeke's restless behaviour, her procrastination over choice of clothes, lipstick, stockings, are part of a search for her true identity. "I'm only an actress," she says in one of the film's few lines, and *It's Me* is a tribute to the performer's resilience, to her ability to retain her appeal under the closest examination. Few actresses could have done so well as Willeke van Ammelrooy here, sensuous, languorous, voluptuous in each and every close-up. The music, too, is mesmeric, sucking one inexorably into a claustrophobic nether region where fantasy and reality collide in a furtive embrace. And even *People '74* has its logical place in Zwartjes's *oeuvre*. "Until now," he says of this documentary about the maimed victims of a war in Guinea-Bissae, "my films were absurd. Now I have made a film about an absurd world." Between such sorties into the irrational areas of the human mind, Frans Zwartjes leads a sane and helpful life, teaching students at the Free Academy Psychopolis, a film workshop in The Hague, and enjoying his family.

E. GEORGE SLUIZER

George Sluizer learnt the craft of film in the traditional Dutch manner, assisting Bert Haanstra on *Fanfare,* and then, for Shell, making *Hold Back the Sea,* concerned with the reclamation of low-lying areas around the Zuiderzee. But there was always an unquiet spirit seething beneath the formalism of Sluizer's documentaries. *Clair Obscur* (1963) has the air of an *avant-garde,* experimental film, with the

Joffre Soares (right) in JOÃO

ambivalent hero stalking the polders with a microphone, trying to capture the sounds of birds and cattle. Then it gradually develops a subtle flavour, and a logic, that remains controlled to the end. A storm breaks and the young man finds himself hemmed in on all sides by dikes and water. Nature, as in van der Horst's *Pan,* seems to be wreaking revenge on this intruder into her privacy. The richly-tinted colour, the sombre clarinet accompaniment, and some quicksilver editing combine to create an arresting short.

Soon Sluizer was to become the new generation's "Flying Dutchman," working in Ireland, Scotland, the Middle East, and Brazil. Born in Paris, he was a merchant seaman during his teens, and grew fascinated by the cultures, and incensed by the hardships, of the Third World. The subject for *João* (*João en het mes,* 1972) was suggested to him by a Portuguese friend. Sluizer fell in love with Odylo Costa's novel, and he and his wife set up the production in Brazil. So instinctive is Sluizer's grasp of the pace, superstitions, and myths of Latin-American life, that he might well be a member of the *cinema nôvo* movement. The film is a dark morality tale about an elderly Indian, João, who boldly chooses a young wife, and then leaves her side to seek his fortune in the Amazonas. When he returns and finds her with a child that could scarcely be his, he lets her know that he will kill her, with a knife. João, played by the distinguished Joffre Soares, is the pillar of the film. His fierce independence, his frugality, and his stubborn self-confidence rule the early scenes. As he accumulates his wealth in the Amazonas, however, João changes. He spends money lavishly. His jealousy becomes a throbbing obsession. Eventually he is rejected as a harbinger of catastrophe by friends and relatives alike.

Sluizer narrates this story with an accomplished ease, making the best possible use of the landscape, and the sounds of the countryside. Some episodes, such as the brawl in a tavern, and the irremediable conflict of death and ecstasy at the end, are genuinely engrossing. But for most of the film, it is the implication of menace, of anger barely concealed, that holds one's attention. And the plight of João is universal. "Wounds heal," he says, "but pain goes on." João becomes a fugitive from the pages of classical tragedy, an Othello whose Iago is his own self-righteousness run amok.

While in Brazil, Sluizer also completed four documentaries. One of these, *The Raft,* about a family's perilous journey down river in order to sell earthenware and other merchandise, won an award at Cracow in 1973. *Letters* is a shorter film, about adults learning to write for the first time, and *Zeca* is the portrait of a Vaqueiro (cowherd) on a social, professional, and domestic level. The last film made by Sluizer during this fruitful sojourn was *Three Days' Respite,* which evokes the exuberant atmosphere of a carnival in a small town.

In the past five years, Sluizer has become even more committed to the cause of the underprivileged. *Land of the Fathers,* focusing on two Palestinian families, was filmed on location in Lebanon; and more recently Sluizer has been involved in a documentary about the manipulation of basic foodstuffs by Capitalism and Communism alike. "I've progressed beyond the Dutch tradition of movie-making," he maintains. "Form can so easily predominate over content. Films, after all, must have a sense not only of the viewer but also of those in front of the cameras."

F. ROLF ORTHEL

Rolf Orthel adheres to the same documentary principles as Johan van der Keuken. He conceives of the film-maker as participant rather than as Olympian observer. His films are journalistic in the investigative sense of that term. Most striking of the Orthel documentaries is *Shadow of a Doubt (Een schijn van twijfel,* 1975). Off-screen, Orthel relates how he grew up in wartime Holland, and how he became more and more absorbed in the experience of those connected with the Nazi death camps. Westerbork was a Dutch camp for German Jews; from there they were transported to Auschwitz and the gas chambers. Orthel tracks down some of the former villains; one defends his failure to protest, claiming that a single man's conscience could hardly have changed the circumstances; another, a doctor, responds to

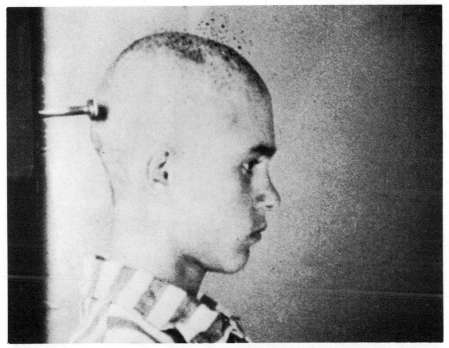

A child in Auschwitz (circa 1941). From SHADOW OF A DOUBT, directed by Rolf Orthel

questions blandly and dispassionately, with a cabinet of surgical instruments at his back, like a sinister token of the past.

Orthel's film appeared almost twenty years after Resnais's *Night and Fog,* and there are the same unnerving switches from the monochrome images of the war to the "real" colours of the present day. There is the same gravity of tone, as Orthel concludes that even the last line of self-defence—ignorance—was denied to the prisoners of Auschwitz. "The past recedes, and turns into stone," he comments as his camera watches the jagged, irregular memorials in the German snow, and Mozart's Rondo in A Minor ripples poignantly on the soundtrack. Apart from this final sequence, Orthel's film eschews the lyrical mood; his anger, an anger directed at all those who feigned want of collusion for so long, is barely hidden. Closely related to *Shadow of a Doubt* is *Dr. Eduard Wirths, Standortarzt Auschwitz,* which examines the life and conscience of a Nazi doctor who committed suicide in prison after the war.

G. LODEWIJK DE BOER

The tall, waxen-faced lover in several of Zwartjes's short films is Lodewijk de Boer, who is also known in the Netherlands for his stage work. *The Family* (1974) is a screen version of his own play, and is a remarkably isolated phenomenon in Dutch cinema. Owing much to

Still from THE FAMILY

Genet and Beckett, and before them to Strindberg, *The Family* deals with human beings who rend and lacerate each other almost involuntarily. Doc and Kil live with their sister in a dilapidated house on the fringes of Amsterdam (although an opening crane shot, over a studio landscape, emphasises the insignificance of the setting), and pounce with eerie malice on any intruder from the outside world, whether he be banker or mere relative from the turgid past. The dialogue is rich in verbal thrusts and feints, but it is de Boer's uncanny sense of the cinematic that is so gripping. His choice of camera angles, his manipulation of sound effects, and his direction of players, are flawless.

The Family is a movie about dreams and futility, about humiliation and frenzy, and in each of the catatonic personalities there is a fragment of oneself reflected. It runs from start to finish with a mad energy that perfectly transmits the "family's" will to keep reality at bay, whatever the cost. This is the kind of subterranean nightmare that Zwartjes himself might have concocted. Meanwhile, Lodewijk de Boer should be urged to continue his journey to the depths of cinema.

9. ANIMATION

In spite of a great tradition in the plastic arts, there has until recently in the Netherlands been little concerted achievement in the field of animation. Two pioneers are outstanding: Joop Geesink and Marten Toonder. Joop and his brother Wim Geesink launched their business in outdoor and film advertising in 1922, and Joop's puppet films won almost a hundred prizes in the postwar period. He created the famous "Dollywood" studios, using every type of stop-motion process: model and photo animation, puppet films, cartoons, and paper dolls. One of his most conspicuous successes was *The Big Four in Conference* (*De grote vier,* 1947), in which puppet diplomats and politicians engage in a stormy summit meeting reminiscent of Yalta. Outside the building, press and camera crews await the outcome of this awesome gathering. "They're all agreed," says the communique at last, "that you can't do better than buy from Holland!" *Kermesse Fantastique,* made around the same time, for Philips, with music by Georges Auric, glitters with bright colours as a man is taken on a ride through space to some celestial funfair. The richness of the gadgetry, and the liveliness of movement, enable this little film to survive the years.

Marten Toonder devoted more energy to cartoons than to puppet films, and during the Fifties produced such engaging shorts as *The Golden Fish* (*De gouden vis,* 1951) and *Moonglow* (1955). Harold Mack, who directed the latter film, used classical characters such as Pierrot, Pierrette, Harlequin, and Columbine to invoke the atmosphere of the "Commedia dell'Arte," with the emotions suggested through music and mime. But Mack is dead now, and Henk Kabos and Cor Icke, two of Geesink's veteran collaborators, finally retired in 1977.

In 1973, an important event took place: the establishment of "Holland Animation," an association supported by practising Dutch animators, and intended as a means of refining and developing the craft of animation in the Netherlands. The consequences have been spectacular. The Dutch have won major prizes at the leading festivals; their marketing has become sophisticated, with an international audience in mind; and one talent has nourished another, so that there are now at least half-a-dozen world-class animators in the Netherlands. Senior among this burgeoning group is, deservedly, Ronald

Cel from Marten Toonder's THE GOLDEN FISH

Bijlsma, who fought a lone battle for recognition in the late, barren Sixties. *The Duel* (1967), a mini-cartoon under two minutes in length, was "full of sex and death," and earned a good reception at Annecy. *In the Void* (1969) contains some of his best work. Bijlsma painted directly under the camera, using a gouache technique, and the film is given considerable menace by Willem Breuker's musical score. *Brainwash* (1973) describes the overthrow of a totalitarian *régime* by the optimism of a single trombonist. Happiness and creativity are, in Bijlsma's view, indestructible, and in *Brainwash* he has found a graphic pattern and a colour system with which to convey his belief, despite the veiled pessimism of the closing images.

Paul Driessen made his mark as early as 1970. *Little Yoghourt* boasts an unusual style and a quaint pictorial approach. He has worked in Canada with consistent success, too, and in association with another Dutchman, Co Hoedeman (whose own *Sandcastle* shared the top award at Annecy in 1977 and won an Academy Award in 1978). Driessen's *The Killing of an Egg* is a brief, laconic parable about the dangers of crushing someone smaller than oneself. *David*, the other Grand Prix-winner at Annecy, touches on the same issue. Like all great animators, Driessen is in sympathy with the underdog, and David is an individual so tiny that his presence is signalled only when he blows up a balloon, or lets the wind ripple through his hair. His voice, a wonderfully disgruntled, flat English accent, constantly

Cel from Ronald Bijlsma's BRAINWASH

addresses the world in general until it—and its owner—is sanctimoniously flattened by a passerby.

If Driessen's style depends on a tremulous, spidery brand of draughtsmanship, that of Gerrit van Dijk is more voluptuous and three-dimensional, in the tradition almost of M.C. Escher (as is *Between the Lights,* by Jacques Verbeek and Karin Wiertz). *CubeMEN-cube* (1975) traps the human experience within the confines of a couple of cubes. Exhibiting their many different facets, these geometric creatures become faces, mouths, hands etc., according to their needs. They coalesce, travel together, have sex, and eventually, inevitably, engage in war against each other. In this film, as in his later *Sportflesh* (1976) and *Quod Libet* (1977), van Dijk is continually changing the image before one's eyes; nothing remains the same for more than a second or so. The small boy grasping a football in *Sportflesh* mutates alarmingly into a whole series of sporting colours and guises, each uglier than the last, until the sportfiend himself is transformed into a football, and the film has turned full circle.

Animation in Europe is an individual's art, and Niek Reus, who studied anthropology, belongs to no school or studio. His *Cartoon (Tekenfilm,* 1974) was selected for the Annecy festival, and is really a meditation on the cartoonist's profession. A little man is drawn to life on an artist's sketchpad, only to be pursued by a belligerent eraser. His creator resorts to "inking in" his outline so that he may not be rubbed into oblivion. *Self-Portrait* shows a face's constituent

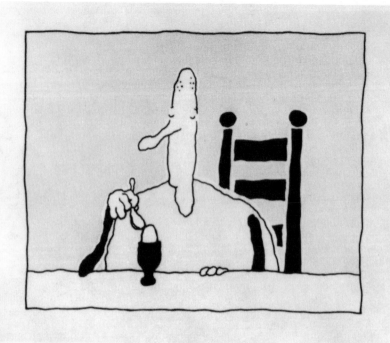

Cel from Paul Driessen's THE KILLING OF AN EGG

features—ears, nose, eyes, moustache—engaged in a merry dance and struggle with one another. A similar conceit lies behind *Latex Amatex* (1976), directed by Bas Beima and Dennis van Boven. Mask-like faces shift and fluctuate in split-screen profusion. Human figures and gestures are realistically and fluently traced. As the title suggests, this film has a sensual quality enhanced by its pastel colouring.

Many other examples of Dutch animation are worthy of note. *Butterfly R.I.P.* (1973) is a neat, single-background comment by Peter Brouwer and Gerrit van Dijk on ecological stupidity, as houses and factories multiply remorselessly, restricting and finally obliterating the liberty of a butterfly. *Thready Games* (directed by Tvika Oren in 1975) introduces two wriggling lengths of twine that writhe against a multi-coloured background. *Weird Bird* (1976) is a talented tale of non-conformism by Delphine de Pury, emphasising yet again that animators in Holland discern, somewhat better than their "live action" colleagues, the dangers of a society in which everyone has the same size and attitudes. *Mister X* (1969) is a Cocteau-like cartoon that traces the Seven Ages of Man and the undeniable circle that runs between birth and death. Rupert van der Linden's design is rich and flowing, a combination of hard-outline characters and softer, half-tone backdrops.

Top left: BUTTERFLY RIP. Top right: Niek Reuss's A TASTE OF HAPPINESS. Lower left: Rupert van der Linden's THE FLOWERS. Lower right: Gerrit van Dijk's cubeMENcube.

Nico Crama (see Chapter Five) spent five years establishing the image of "Holland Animation" outside the Netherlands. Like other short films, cartoons qualify for grants from the Ministry of Culture, Recreation and Social Welfare. "Subsidy alone is no longer sufficient," commented Crama. "What we need now is long-term planning, guidance, and above all stimulation for the film-makers to co-operate among themselves. Everyone is so involved in his own work that the building up of a sort of national tradition is neglected." Nevertheless, by their efforts during the past few years, Dutch animators have demonstrated that their work is often more commercially viable and attractive than live action shorts, which do not reach the cinemas so frequently. The technique of animation is well taught at the Rietveld Academy in Amsterdam, the Free Academy Psychopolis in The Hague, and at courses in colleges such as the Volksuniversiteit in Groningen. Cineco, one of Holland's largest film laboratories, has expanded its facilities to include an "Optical Art

House," with the most modern cameras and equipment for animators. Encouraged by an increasing number of festival awards, Dutch animation is definitely progressing faster than any other area of film-making in Holland. Perhaps within the *next* five years, a full-length animated production will be feasible.

10. ALTERNATIVE CINEMA AND TELEVISION TALENTS

The "alternative cinema" movement is international in composition and national in effect. There are, after all, social and economic grievances lurking in even the most affluent of countries, and the intensity of effort by radical Dutch directors is accentuated by the limited size of the Netherlands, and by the sophisticated means of distribution that have been formed in opposition to the commercial circuits adhering to the Nederlandse Bioscoopbond. Producers, distributors, and cinema-owners are united within this association and no member may do business with a non-member; hence the need for a separate 16mm circuit.

In Holland, the polemicist has two principal choices of expression: television, or the alternative circuit, which comprises the "Film Houses" (established in all the main towns and cities) and various groups and societies with projection facilities. Film International in Rotterdam, and Fugitive Cinema in Amsterdam, are in the vanguard of this latter movement, and have managed to distribute several foreign films that might never otherwise have been screened in the Netherlands. While Film International concentrates on features with social and aesthetic significance, Fugitive places the emphasis on documentaries (although its catalogue includes, among other titles, Bertolucci's *Strategia del ragno* and Troell's *Ole dole doff*). Fugitive releases and generally nourishes the celebrated "Amsterdams Stadsjournaal," a series of controversial inquiries on film that appear at the rate of about seven per year, and are rented out to unions and institutions of further education. Each of these "city newsreels" runs for about twenty minutes in black-and-white, and focuses on cracks and abuses in the country's social system. There's a strong sense of teamwork here, and volunteers gravitate to the Stadsjournaal from universities, from the radical film magazine, "Skrien," and from the ranks of the movie professionals (e.g. Theo van der Sand, who was cameraman on Nouchka van Brakel's *The Début*).

Annette Apon and the crew of the "Amsterdams Stadsjournaal" shooting in the streets of the capital

Most of these broadsheets consist of a mixture of interviews and documentary sequences. In issue number 10, for example, *Scenes from a Soldier's Life,* one sees a platoon drilling without enthusiasm on a parade ground, while a protest march demands freedom for the VVDM, the soldiers' union in the Netherlands. The film underlines the need for an amateur army; if it were professional, the men themselves insist that the danger of a military *coup* would be enhanced. Number 7 denounces the inexorable growth of monopolism in the Dutch bakery industry. Some 90% of the industry is owned by just four companies. The newsreel uses titles to show, one after another like kidnap victims, the names of the firms absorbed by the consortia. Control, argues the Stadsjournaal, must pass to the Dutch people.

Some of the group's newsreels are impaired by the presence of professional actors. In Number 13, devoted to Dutch high schools and their role as launch-pads for the universities, there is an artificial mood in the scenes that re-create college life. Without doubt the Stadsjournaals work most effectively when, like the Cuban newsreels, they bombard the spectator with a flurry of interviews, songs, diagrams, and titles. Each film is preceded by a lengthy period of research, and members of the team switch duties; Annette Apon, who translated some of the Dutch dialogue for me, said that she had

worked in practically all capacities save editing. The group's prime
aim is to make films that can really be *used* by various organisations,
and not just languish in a political vacuum. Propagandist their reports
may be, but they have a punch lacking in many more respectable
Dutch documentaries.

*   *   *

The films released by Fugitive and other non-commercial groups
are assured of a public already disposed to political commitment.
Radicalism, however, is far more of a luxury where television is
concerned, especially in the Netherlands, where a broadcasting
station must maintain a minimum "membership" level of 100,000
people—people who subscribe to the station regularly because they
admire its programmes. VPRO is one of seven national TV companies permitted to make use of the country's two channels. At
present they have the support of 180,000 "members," and their
programmes contrive to be both challenging and entertaining. Not
surprisingly, the staff of around a hundred at VPRO (plus many
more freelance directors) include some of the most talented of Dutch
film-makers. Jan Blokker, Associate Director of the station, is a
former critic and screenwriter (he collaborated on Haanstra's *Fanfare*
and on some of the most adventurous Dutch films of the Sixties). He
explains the traditional demarcation lines between TV stations in
Holland; and now VPRO began life in the Thirties and Forties as a
representative of Liberal Protestant sentiments. But the old loyalties
were under fiercer and fiercer pressure as the national mood changed
in keeping with the spirit of the Sixties. At the end of that decade, a
new group of directors arrived at VPRO. Tens of thousands of
conservative "members" were lost. Directors like Johan van der
Keuken (see Chapter Eight) revived the cinematic indignation of
Joris Ivens. VPRO, insists Blokker, must be as flexible and dynamic as
possible without lapsing into dogmatism. The form of the documentaries produced by this lively station is sober and unadorned. "Style
can so often be a means of escaping the issue, and so we seek to avoid
that," he says. Since 1972, VPRO has won the Critics' Prize for the
Best Programme on Dutch television every year.

Hans Keller is among the most resourceful and experienced of the
VPRO house directors. He likes to use extracts from other TV
programmes as the raw material with which to deliver a stinging
attack on such subjects as "Muzak," the American canned music
phenomenon that is now a multi-million dollar industry with its own
pretentious jargon and an almost messianic desire to convert the rest
of the world to an acceptance of its saccharine bliss. Keller is also
responsible for a regular series entitled *The Gap of Holland,* consisting
of quirkish news items that would normally never reach the TV
screen.

Another provocative film-maker at VPRO is Wim Schippers, who for many years worked in association with Wim van der Linden, and whose 1973 Christmas show caused a furore in the Netherlands. The programme began with naked girls singing lustily in a crowded coach, with a cheerful pastor in attendance. In the wake of this flagrant ridicule of the established church, thousands of viewers cancelled their subscription to VPRO. But the station soon recovered its lost members, for not all of its programmes are outrageous (e.g. the several studies of modern Dutch history, each three hours in length). Profiles of Iceland at the time of the Cod War, and of the conservative community of Pella, Iowa, which was founded more than a century ago by migrant Dutch folk, have helped to sustain the place of VPRO at the forefront of television in the Netherlands. Recently, another group known simply as EO has achieved the minimum 100,000 membership demanded as a qualification for nationwide broadcasting. The directors at EO are dissident, somewhat right-wing in their attitudes, and have not attracted a committed audience in the same way as VPRO did a decade earlier. Perhaps it is true to say that the Dutch, like the Swedes, are more willing to accept a political challenge in their drawing rooms than they are in a movie theatre. There is an undeniably *modern* quality to TV, both technologically and aesthetically, while the cinema still labours under the burden of its popcorn duty merely to divert.

How fortunate are the Dutch, to enjoy such freedom in TV and cinema! Freedom of expression. Freedom, in truth, from the ruthless exigencies of commercial cinema. Of course, Dutch producers still go bankrupt from time to time. A director in Holland, however, *can* obtain financial sustenance for even the most controversial of projects; and he *can* survive to make another film should his first effort prove a catastrophe at the box-office. There are not many national film industries of which that can be said. The Dutch cinema has not yet produced its Bergman, its Dreyer, its Wajda, or its Buñuel, but its benevolent, mixed-economy system ensures that, with each new feature, it is more and more likely to do so.

BIBLIOGRAPHY

1. Fens, Kees. "Twenty Years of Dutch Literature, Some Trends and Central Figures" (Ministry of Cultural Affairs, Recreation, and Social Welfare, Rijswijk, 1973).
2. Van Nooten, S.I. "Contributions of Dutchmen to the Beginnings of Film Technology," in "International Film Guide 1973" (Tantivy Press, London; A.S. Barnes, New York, 1972).
3. Donaldson, Geoffrey. "De nederlandse zwijgende films en de nederlandse 'filmhistorici'," in "Skrien" (Amsterdam, September, 1970), and "De erste nederlandse speelfilms en de gebroeders Mullens," in "Skrien" (Amsterdam, January, 1972).
4. Ivens, Joris. "The Camera and I" (International Publishers, New York; Seven Seas Books, Berlin, 1969).
5. Saaltink, Hans. "Dutch Cinema: Old Guard, New Guard, Avant-Garde," in "Delta" (Amsterdam, Winter 1967-68).
6. Visscher, Dr. H.S. "The Lucid Eye: Johan van der Keuken" (United Netherlands Film Institute/Skoop, Amsterdam, 1973).
7. Stuiveling, Garmt. "A Sampling of Dutch Literature" (Radio Nederland Wereldomroep, Hilversum, 196?).
8. Boost, Charles. "Dutch Art Today: Film" (Contact, Amsterdam, 1957).
9. Cowie, Peter. "Dutch Films," in "Film Quarterly" (Berkeley, California, Winter 1965-66).
10. Milo, Otto. "Animation in Holland," in "International Film Guide 1977" (Tantivy Press, London; A.S. Barnes, New York, 1976).

Note: there is also much valuable source material to be found in the illustrated booklets issued at biennial or triennial intervals by the Ministry of Cultural Affairs, Recreation and Social Welfare under the title of "Dutch Film"; in the bulletins of "Holland Animation"; in the Dutch film magazines, "Skoop" and "Skrien"; in the brochures prepared for sales purposes by the RVD (Netherlands Information Service); and in occasional issues of the KLM in-flight magazine, "Holland Herald."

FILMOGRAPHIES

JACOB BIJL

For nine years Bijl was a freelance director and producer of documentary films, mostly for television. His first featurette was *Jealousy* (1974), starring his wife, Jessamin Stärcke, who also has a leading role in his major work, *Scrim* (1976), in which she co-starred with Geraldine Chaplin. *Scrim* was selected for screening by many international festivals, and went out on both Swedish and West German television. Bijl is one of the few young Dutch directors to emphasise the psychological drama of everyday life. His latest film is *Tiro*.

Ronald Bijlsma

Jacob Bijl

RONALD BIJLSMA

Born Rotterdam 1934. Studied at the Academy of Arts in Rotterdam, concentrating on stained glass and etching. In 1957, he turned to animation and joined the Marten Toonder Studio. In 1961, he began working with the American director Jim Hiltz at Cinecentrum in Hilversum. Six years later he launched his own company, producing commercials and TV-leaders, working with well-known designers such as Bruce Meek, Keith McEwan, and Heinz Edelmann. Bijlsma's big breakthrough came in 1967, when his first "free" film, *The Duel*, only two minutes long, was screened at Annecy. In 1969, he made *In the Void*, painted directly under the camera using a gouache technique, and this film subsequently made the rounds of eighteen international festivals. In 1973, Bijlsma produced his most ambitious animated work to date, *Brainwash*, a satire on a society of the future. Since then he has concentrated on TV work and cut-out techniques of animation.

NOUCHKA VAN BRAKEL

Born Amsterdam 1940. During the Sixties, she studied at the Netherlands Film Academy, and assisted on various key films (e.g. *Joszef Katús*, where she also played a small role). One of the few women directors to emerge during this period, she has been attracted by educational problems and the experiences of

Nouchka van Brakel

140

the very young and the very old. After her *début* in 1967 with a children's film entitled *Sabotage,* she found an international market with the freewheeling, sun-laden *Baby in the Tree* (1969). In the early Seventies, she specialised in television work (e.g. *One Has to Go On Looking,* 1971), and in 1975 her segment of the four *Melancholy Tales* was released. In 1977 she won critical praise, and a major award at the Cairo Film Festival, for her first feature, *The Début,* which showed her to be among the most intelligent and perspicacious film-makers of her generation in the Netherlands. In 1978 she started to direct *A Woman Like Eve,* starring Maria Schneider and Monique van de Ven, and released in 1979.

(1970), and Jan Oonk's *Marble* 1970), and the cartoons *Butterfly 1975* (1973), *cubeMENcube* (1975), and *Sportflesh* (1976). In his own work as director, he reveals a marked preference for subjects related to the arts and literature: *Photo-Portrait* (1970), *Daumier, Eye-Witness of an Epoch* (1971), and *Piet Mondriaan* (1973) are typical examples of his craft. Recently, Crama has been working and living in Canada, where he has directed a one-hour documentary on the Dutch-Canadians for the National Film Board.

ADRIAAN DITVOORST

Born Bergen-op-Zoom 1940. Graduated, like all the most important young Dutch film-makers, from the Netherlands Film

Nico Crama

Adriaan Ditvoorst

NICO CRAMA

Born Leiden 1935. Started filming while still at preparatory school. Later studied and worked in Paris and Amsterdam. Began film career at the Dutch Educational Film Foundation in The Hague, first as an editor, later as a scriptwriter/director of educational films. In 1961, Crama became an independent producer. His first short, *Netsuke* (1961), is still shown regularly. Apart from directing, he has produced several shorts, both live-action and animated, and until recently was executive of the Holland Animation group. Crama's productions include Paul Verhoeven's *The Wrestler*

Academy. His first short, *That Way to Madra* (1965), won prizes at five film festivals including Chicago and Mannheim. Much attracted to the claustrophobic novels and stories of W.F. Hermans, he made *Paranoia* (1967), from a work by that author. *Antenna* (1969) followed, starring the then-fashionable actor, Pierre Clémenti, and another adaptation from Hermans, *The Blind Photographer* (1972). In 1975, he released *Flanagan,* a family drama worked out on classical lines, and in 1978 caused some controversy with his satire, *The Cloak of Charity.* Ditvoorst has also worked for television with an adaptation of Camus's *La chute* to his credit.

John Ferno

Mannus Franken

JOHN FERNO

Born Bergen (NH) 1918. Real name: John Fernhout. Joined Joris Ivens at an incredibly young age, and was cameraman on such classics as *Spanish Earth*. With Henri Storck, he made a notable short about the gigantic statues on Easter Island. Ferno has worked in almost as many lands as Ivens—Canada, the United States, the West Indies, Africa, Israel, and most European countries. Two of his most spectacular shorts are *Fortress of Peace* (1965), about the Swiss army on manoeuvres, and *Sky over Holland* (1967), which won the Grand Prix at Cannes. Both these films were in 70mm. In 1971 Ferno made *The Tree of Life,* a study of the Jews and the Diaspora. His son, Douwes, is a gifted cinematographer in his own right.

MANNUS FRANKEN

Born Deventer 1899, died Lochem 1953. One of the most underrated of all Dutch film-makers, Franken was in fact a true pioneer and a very real pillar of the documentary achievement usually credited solely to Joris Ivens. An actor and journalist in his early days, and a student of economics, he began writing film criticism in the mid-Twenties and was soon doing screenplays for Ivens. One of the founders of the "Filmliga," the first Dutch film society, Franken collaborated closely on *Breakers.* His own films include

Jardin du Luxembourg (with H.J. Ankersmit, 1929), *Wind in the Sails* (with W.L. Leclerq, 1934), *Pareh, Song of the Rice* (1935), and *Tanah Sabrang* (1938), both shot in Indonesia. Franken is also known as the founder of the most famous art-house in Holland, "De Uitkijk" in Amsterdam.

LOUIS A. VAN GASTEREN

Born Amsterdam 1922. Van Gasteren comes from an acting family. At first he studied electronics in order to experiment with audio-visual methods in the theatre, and switched to film-making as a

Louis van Gasteren

career in 1947. He specialised in sound engineering in Paris, and did his first work on newsreels in Holland. In 1950 he founded his own company, Spectrum Film, in Amsterdam. Van Gasteren's most admired documentaries include *Brown Gold* (co-directed with van Haren Noman, 1952), *Railplan 68* (1954), and *Report from Biafra* (1968), for which he obtained the Dutch State Award for Film Art. He has never been fully satisfied with the documentary *genre,* however, as *Stranding* (1956, a thriller) and *The House* (1962) clearly indicate. In recent years he has spent more and more of his energy on experimental work involving human perception and audio-visual techniques. His television documentaries are always taut and affecting.

BERT HAANSTRA

Born Holten 1916. Although fascinated by Chaplin and Lloyd in his teens, Haanstra started out as a painter and poster designer. He was given his chance as cameraman on Paul Bruno Schreiber's *Myrthe en de demonen* (1948) and shortly afterwards made a delightful little short, *The Muiden Circle Lives Again* (with costumes designed by his wife). His first public success was *Mirror of Holland,* winner of the Grand Prix at Cannes in 1950, and since then he has directed over twenty films, six of them features. Among his more famous shorts are *Rembrandt, Painter of Men* (1956), *Glass*

(1958), *Zoo* (1962), and the Shell-sponsored documentary, *The Rival World* (1954). Haanstra has his own laboratory facilities at his home in Laren, and is the most famous of all contemporary Dutch directors. His features include the very successful *Fanfare* (1959), made in collaboration with Mackendrick, the award-winning *The Human Dutch* (1963), *The Voice of the Water* (1966), *Ape and Super-Ape* (1973), and the intriguing psychological study, *When the Poppies Bloom Again* (1975).

MAX DE HAAS

Born Amsterdam 1905. One of the veterans of Dutch film. Launched his own company (Visie Film) in 1933, and proceeded to make over a hundred documentaries and 1,600 subjects for international film and television newsreels. His *Ballad of the Top Hat* (1936) is considered a minor classic and a precursor of "neo-realism." During the Second World War, he was sent to the Dutch East Indies to make films stressing the Nazi and Japanese danger. Other fine de Haas films include *Maskerage* (1952), which won various awards, *Days of My Years* (1960), and *Dream without End* (1964). Many young Dutch directors have served their apprenticeship with de Haas, and his unostentatious achievements form part of the backbone of Dutch documentary.

Bert Haanstra

Max de Haas

Theo van Haren Noman

Nikolai van der Heyde

THEO VAN HAREN NOMAN

Born Amsterdam 1917. After secondary school, he went to England where he took a course of technical training. It was not until after the Second World War that he entered the film field, joining Polygoon-Profilti, which produced the Dutch newsreel and documentaries. For five years, van Haren Noman worked in this organisation as a cameraman; then he turned freelance, making *Brown Gold* (1952) jointly with Louis van Gasteren, about cocoa and chocolate manufacture. He also made a number of other documentaries in Africa, as well as several films for the government and commercial enterprises. In 1955, he was chief commercial television cameraman for the E 55 Exhibition in Rotterdam. Besides his sponsored films, van Haren Noman has made at least two notable "free" shorts, *An Army of Hewn Stone* (1957), an evocation of the tragedies of war through a series of shots of statues and memorials, and *The Injured Man* (1966), an hallucinatory, subjective view of a hospital through the eyes of a dying patient.

NIKOLAI VAN DER HEYDE

Born Leeuwarden 1935. Studied at the Netherlands Film Academy, and wrote and directed *Bowling Alley* (1963) even before completing his course. This film received a prize at the Cinestud student festival. His first feature, *A Morning of Six Weeks* (1966), was much influenced by the French nouvelle vague, and bore witness to van der Heyde's assiduous training beside such directors as Chabrol and Donen. *To Grab the Ring* (1968) was less successful, and it was only with *Love Comes Quietly . . .* (1973) that he achieved genuine recognition from critics and public alike in Holland. *Help, the Doctor's Drowning!* (1974), was visually ravishing, and was, like the previous film, photographed by the Swedish cinematographer, Jörgen Persson. Ven der Heyde is in many ways the most sensitive of the new Dutch directors, and none has improvised so successfully as he has, in the vein of Cassavetes and Truffaut.

HERMAN VAN DER HORST

Born Kinderdijk 1911, died Vogelenzang 1976. After pursuing a commercial education, he took up biological studies as curator of a museum, and specialized in nature photography. In 1945, he made his first film, *Metamorphosis*, which attracted considerable attention at the Cannes Festival, and his next work, *Tarnished Land* (1946), won an award in Locarno. During the Fifties, van der Horst became celebrated for his vibrant editing and for his uncanny attunement to the natural world, in such documentaries as *Shoot the Nets* (1952), *Steady!* (1953), *Praise the Sea* (1958), and *Faja*

144

Herman van der Hors

Lobbi (this last a full-length film shot in colour in Surinam, 1959). In 1964, he shot *Amsterdam,* and four years later completed his final film, *Toccata* (1968), about the organ in the Grote Kerk in Amsterdam, with its remarkable playing by Feike Asma. Van der Horst was one of the most meticulous, painstaking craftsmen in the history of the Dutch cinema.

ROB HOUWER

Born The Hague 1937. Studied at the Deutsches Institut für Film und Fernsehen in Munich. First caught attention at the age of twenty-one with his short, *Dog Days.* During the early Sixties he made prize-winning shorts in the Netherlands, among them *The Key* (1963), and *Application* (1964). Then he moved to West Germany and established a production company there. Houwer was responsible for Volker Schlöndorff's *Mord und Totschlag* and other significant films of the German new wave. At the turn of the decade, however, he returned to Holland, and, working with the director Paul Verhoeven, embarked on a series of feature films that collectively have earned more money than could ever have been imagined on the Dutch market: *Business Is Business, Turkish Delight, Cathy Tippel,* and *Soldier of Orange (Survival Run).* He is the most successful producer in Holland.

HATTUM HOVING

Born Delft 1918, died 1976. Joined the film industry in 1945, making his *début* as a director with *Go Out into the World* (1950). Specialised in documentaries about science and industry, and at his best transcended his material through an uncanny brilliance of technique and philosophical intuition. His finest shorts include *Os Mundi* (1960), *Interludium Electronicum* (1964), and the lyrical *Sailing* (1963), which has sold more prints than almost any Dutch film save *Glass.* In *Mixummerdaydream* (1968), and *Light* (1971) he experimented with colour shifts and solarisation techniques. Hov-

Rob Houwer

Hattum Hoving

ing belongs with Haanstra, van der Horst, and Ferno in the vanguard of Dutch postwar documentarists.

JORIS IVENS

Born Nijmegen 1898. The most celebrated of all Dutch film-makers, he began his career as a director with a short entitled *The Bridge* (1928). Then followed *Rain* (1929), *Breakers* (1929), *Borinage* (1933), *New Earth* (1934), *Spanish Earth* (1937), *The 400 Million* (1938), *Indonesia Calling* (1946), *La Seine a rencontré Paris* (1957), *A Valparaiso* (1963), *Rotterdam-Europoort* (1965), *Le*

Hans Keller

Joris Ivens

United States, and has been supervising editor of such documentary series as *The Gap of the Netherlands* and *Zorgvliedt*. Received the Nipkov Disc, a Dutch TV award, in 1973. Keller has continued to write criticism for daily and weekly newspapers and journals.

JOHAN VAN DER KEUKEN

Born Amsterdam 1938. Began his career while extremely young, as a photographer, and published three books of photographs, "We Are 17" (1955), "Behind Glass" (1957), and "Paris Mortel" (1963). From 1956 to 1958 he attended a

17eme parallele (1968), and the mighty series, *How Yukong Moved the Mountains* (1976), to name but a few of the many documentaries Ivens has made. Virtually all his films are politically committed in content and style, and Ivens is more an international film-maker than a Dutch one. But for many of the younger directors in Holland he has proved to be both idol and mentor.

HANS KELLER

Born Haarlem 1937. Became a journalist and television critic after completing his military service. Has been a television producer/director for various broadcasting stations (and especially VPRO) since 1963. He has devised literary programmes, an experimental film series, a series of documentaries about the

Johan van der Keuken

course in film-making at IDHEC in Paris, wrote film criticism for a Dutch weekly paper, and since 1959 has made close to thirty films, most of them produced for television. Among van der Keuken's boldest, most experimental documentaries are *Blind child* (1964), *A Film for Lucebert* (1967), *The Spirit of the Time* (1968), *Beauty* (a fantasy, 1970), *Diary* (1972), *The Reading Lesson* (1973), *The New Ice-Age* (1974), *The Palestinians* (1975), and *The Flat Jungle* (1978), which won a major award at the Nyon Festival. Van der Keuken is among the most widely-travelled of all Dutch film-makers.

CHARLES HUGUENOT VAN DER LINDEN

Born Amsterdam 1909. Like Haanstra, he grew up in a painter's family, of French and Swiss origin. In the Twenties he worked for Paramount and prepared Dutch versions of numerous American films. His work took him to Berlin and Paris, and it was 1935 before he made his first independent feature, *Young Hearts,* which was screened at the Venice Festival. After the war, van der Linden established a company of his own (his wife acting as producer), and made a stream of films, among them the documentary on the consequences of the flood disasters of 1953, *View of Middelharnis. Interlude by Candlelight* was about

Charles Huguenot van der Linden

the life and work of an aged puppet-maker, and *Big City Blues* was an experimental fiction film in the style of Stan Brakhage. *The Building Game* (1963) and *This Tiny World* (which won him an Academy Award in Hollywood in 1973) are among his finest documentaries.

René van Nie

RENÉ VAN NIE

Born Overschie 1938. Began as apprentice to Max de Haas. Was attached to Cinecentrum in Hilversum for many years before becoming a freelance, first as a cameraman, then as scriptwriter and director. Van Nie has made a large number of shorts on assignment and for television, including *At Eye Level* (1965), *Holland* (1968), and *A Woman in the Arts.* In 1969 he caused a stir with his film about an old soldier's home, *Bronbeek for Example,* and in 1971 he turned to fictional film-making with the scope film, *Blackmail.* But van Nie's talent only came to the fore with his features in the mid-Seventies, notably *Anna, Child of the Daffodils* (1975), and *A Silent Love* (1977). He works independently and believes wholeheartedly in the concept of feature films. His latest production is *A Deadly Sin* (1979).

ROLF ORTHEL

Born The Hague 1936. After leaving school, he attended IDHEC in Paris, where he graduated in 1960. Since then,

Rolf Orthel

Pim de la Parra

Orthel has been a freelance film-maker, concentrating on the investigative documentary. *Red Cross on White Field* (1967) was commissioned by the Dutch Red Cross on the occasion of its centenary, and the facts that he discovered about the Red Cross in wartime led Orthel to embark on *Shadow of a Doubt* (1975), an essay about the concentration camps and how people try to recall or obliterate the memories of those hideous institutions. Closely related to *Shadow of a Doubt* (which won a top prize at the Oberhausen Festival) is *Dr. Eduard Wirths, Standortarzt Auschwitz* (1975), a documentary about a German doctor who worked in Auschwitz during the Nazi era. Apart from his own work, Orthel has assisted Bert Haanstra on *The Voice of the Water* and *Ape and Super-Ape*. He also produces films for other directors.

PIM DE LA PARRA

Born Surinam 1940. Studied political and social science at the University of Amsterdam, switched to film, and attended the Netherlands Film Academy. With his close friend, Wim Verstappen, he founded Scorpio Films, a production company that was at the very heart of the feature film movement in Dutch cinema in the late Sixties and early Seventies. His own films as director include *Aah . . . Tamara* (1965), *Obsessions* (1968), *Rubia's Jungle* (1970), and *Frank and Eva, Living*

Apart Together (1974). In 1976 he returned to his native Surinam to shoot *One People*. De la Parra also worked as producer on all Verstappen's films up to 1976. In 1978 he published his autobiography. With his fierce optimism and his unstinted admiration for the American "B" movie, de la Parra is one of the most likeable figures in the Dutch film world.

FONS RADEMAKERS

Born Roosendaal 1920. Studied at the School of Dramatic Art in Amsterdam and, despite the intervention of the Second World War, pursued a career in the theatre at first in Holland, and later in France. In the early Fifties his interest in film-making grew stronger, and he served as assistant to directors such as Renoir, De Sica, and Crichton. His first feature, made in 1958, was *Village on the River,* revealing a highly individual style somewhat reminiscent of Bergman and Torre-Nilsson. This film was nominated for an Academy Award in 1960, and in the same year Rademakers made *That Joyous Eve,* which won a Silver Bear in Berlin. There followed *The Knife* (1961), *The Spitting Image* (1963), *The Dance of the Heron* (1966), *Mira* (1971), *Because of the Cats* (1973), and the monumental *Max Havelaar* (1976), which won a major prize at the Tehran Festival and opened to sensational business in the United States. Rademakers is shooting a feature inspired by a court case in Belgium in 1978.

Fons Rademakers

GEORGE SLUIZER

Born Paris 1932. He studied at IDHEC in Paris, graduating from there in 1956, after which he became an assistant to Bert Haanstra and embarked on his own short films for Shell: *Hold Back the Sea* (1961) and *The World of Chemistry* (1964). He also made the haunting short, *Clair Obscur* (1963). In the later Sixties he began to travel and to make films in various countries. He shot a documentary on Ireland, and several shorts for the National Geographic Society. In

1971 he visited South America and settled in Brazil to make the full-length fictional feature, *João* (1972). He also made a series of four documentaries about aspects of life in the interior of Brazil. Recently he has made his base once more in the Netherlands, and has been shooting *Twice a Woman*, based on a novel by the Dutch author Harry Mulisch, and starring Anthony Perkins, Bibi Andersson and Sandra Dumas. He has also produced films for other directors, notably Herbert Curiël's *Year of the Cancer* (1975).

JOS STELLING

Born Utrecht 1945. Experimented with feature films as an autodidact, and has made a documentary about his native town. Worked for eight years with non-professionals on his much-heralded *début*, the Cannes Festival entry *Mariken van Nieumeghen* (1974). This was soon followed by another feature set in medieval times, *Elckerlyc* (1975). His most ambitious work to date, *Rembrandt fecit 1669* (1977), is a careful reconstruction of the painter's life, viewed in a series of tableaux. Stelling is a genuine experimentalist, each of whose films shows a marked improvement over its predecessor. *Rembrandt fecit 1669* won prizes at Cork and Asolo in 1978.

George Sluizer

Jos Stelling

Paul Verhoeven

Wim Verstappen

PAUL VERHOEVEN

Born Amsterdam 1938. After his secondary education, Verhoeven decided to go to the University of Leiden. With his fellow students there, he made an amateur film, *Een Hagedis Teveel* (1960), which won a prize at the first international student film Festival, Cinestud 1960. This was the basis for a grant by the Ministry of Culture for *Party* (1963), which won a prize at Cork. During his military service in 1965-66, Verhoeven directed a film on the Dutch marines (*Het Korps Mariniers*). Some years of TV work followed, including a series of twelve shorts under the title of *Floris,* a kind of Dutch Ivanhoe. The script for this was written by Gerard Soeteman, with whom Verhoeven has since collaborated. During the Seventies, Verhoeven formed a highly successful partnership with the producer Rob Houwer, with each film making almost more money than the last: *Business Is Business* (1971), *Turkish Delight* (1972), *Cathy Tippel* (1975), and *Soldier of Orange (Survival Run,* 1977).

WIM VERSTAPPEN

Born Gemert 1937. Studied chemistry at the University of Amsterdam, but, like his friend Pim de la Parra, enrolled at the Netherlands Film Academy soon after it had been opened. Co-founded (with de la Parra) the influential film magazine,

"Skoop," and also established Scorpio Films, a production company owned jointly by him and de la Parra. His feature, *Joszef Katús* (1966), made an impression on the festival circuit, and since then his films have included *Confessions of Loving Couples* (1967), *Drop Out* (1969), *Blue Movie* (1970), *VD* (1972), *Dakota* (1974), *Alicia* (1975), and the recently released *Pastorale 1943* (1978), his first feature away from Scorpio and also his most successful from a critical point of view. Verstappen formed with de la Parra one of the most significant partnerships in modern Dutch film, and there is a clearly discernible maturity about his later work.

JAN VRIJMAN

Born Amsterdam 1925. Vrijman worked at first as a journalist, and in 1952 began writing for television. His experimental documentary about the Dutch "action" painter, Karel Appel, won a Golden Bear at Berlin in 1962, and soon afterwards Vrijman established his own company, Cineproductie. He quickly became a focal point of the Dutch "new wave" in the late Sixties, producing such key works as *Illusion Is a Gangster Girl* and *The Enemies* (1967). He was commissioned to create the Dutch pavilion film for Expo 70 in Osaka, and this was a resounding success. In the Seventies he has continued to make idiosyncratic documen-

Jan Vrijman

taries, among them *The Living Neighbourhood, Room to Play* (1972), and *The Making of a Ballet* (1973). His sphere of interest includes studies of social problems, and he produced a documentary on mental deficiency. Vrijman is gifted as a writer and polemicist as well as a director and producer.

FRANS WEISZ

Born Amsterdam 1938. Born of Hungarian and Dutch-Portuguese parents, Weisz studied at the Netherlands Film Academy, and was script-assistant on *A Dog of Flanders* and assistant director on Emmer's *La ragazza in vetrina,* before going in 1960 to attend the Centro Sperimentale film school in Rome. In 1963, with Remco Campert, Weisz made *Heroes in a Rocking Chair.* His first big success came with an extremely imaginative and sensitive sponsored short, *A Sunday on the Island of the Grande Jatte* (1965). He quickly turned to features, but *Illusion is a Gangster Girl* was a disappointment in box-office terms, and it was not until the early Seventies that he was able to find a commercial formula, with two successful comedy-thrillers, *The Burglar* (1972) and *Same Player Shoots Again* (1973). Recently he has found himself much appreciated as a director of commercials for Dutch television.

FRANS ZWARTJES

Born Alkmaar 1927. He studied the violin and played in the orchestra of the Netherlands Opera for five years. He even made violins himself for some time before turning to sculpture, painting, drawing, artefacts, and even "happenings." While teaching experimental design in Eindhoven to feed his family, he began creating an extraordinary series of films. Zwartjes handles every phase of production himself, and to date has made over twenty shorts, all of them highly experimental in a style uniquely his own if also somewhat reminiscent of the American "underground." These shorts, which have been widely screened at festivals and film societies round the world, include *Birds* (1968), *Eating* (1969), *Spare Bedroom, Living* (1971), and the feature-length *It's Me* (1976), starring Willeke van Ammelrooy.

Frans Weisz

Frans Zwartjes

INDEX

(to films cited in the text).